West African Nature Handbooks

General Editor: H. J. Savory, M.Sc.

BIRDS OF THE WEST AFRICAN TOWN AND GARDEN

JOHN H. ELGOOD

M.A., M.B.O.U.

ILLUSTRATED BY ERNEST C. MANSELL

LONGMAN

LONGMAN GROUP LTD
Longman House
Burnt Mill, Harlow,
Essex CM20 2JE,
England

First published 1960
New impressions 1964; 1968; 1972;
*1976; *1979; *1982

ISBN 0 582 60850 3

Other titles in the series

WEST AFRICAN LILIES AND ORCHIDS

WEST AFRICAN SNAKES

SMALL MAMMALS OF WEST AFRICA

WEST AFRICAN BUTTERFLIES AND MOTHS

WEST AFRICAN TREES

In preparation

WEST AFRICAN FRESHWATER FISH

LARGE MAMMALS OF WEST AFRICA

Printed in Hong Kong by
Wah Cheong Printing Press Ltd

LIST OF CONTENTS AND PLATES

PREFACE

In a book of such limited scope as this it has been a matter of great difficulty to select just one hundred birds. The reason for this difficulty is not hard to understand. West Africa is a vast and diverse area. The distance from Bathurst in the Gambia to Lake Chad is approximately 2,000 miles, or about as far as from London to Cairo or from New York to Los Angeles. From the vegetational aspect the area ranges from tropical rain forest in parts of Sierra Leone and southern Nigeria, through a series of different types of savannah to the margins of the Sahara desert. Rainfall may be as high as 400 inches per annum at Debundscha in the Cameroons, or as low as 10 inches at Katsina in northern Nigeria. Clearly birds that are familiar in Accra are not likely to be so in either Freetown or Kano, for, despite their powers of flight, birds, like other animals, are adapted to life in a definite kind of surroundings or environment. This introduces the second major difficulty in selection. Even within a limited area, the environment will vary greatly. This may be due to natural causes such as the presence of a great river, like the Niger or the Volta, or to a change in altitude. On the other hand variations in environment may be due to human activity such as farming, the development of towns with houses and schools and their surrounding gardens and compounds, or the construction of reservoirs for water storage. All of these diverse environments have their associated birds. In selecting the birds for this book the author has therefore had to adopt some definite policy. The policy has been to include only birds which have been seen by him, at some place or another in West Africa, in a garden or compound. In other words all the species included are sufficiently fearless of man to frequent his surroundings. Inevitably the selection, being the author's own, is coloured by his own experiences, largely in southern Nigeria. Nevertheless, widespread kinds of birds have been chosen as far as possible, but many common kinds have been omitted because they are not normally associated with towns and gardens.

Both English and scientific names have been given for the selected species, but no local names, as these are too numerous and not sufficiently exact in many cases. The English and scientific names have been taken from the works of Dr. D. A. Bannerman, the recognised authority on the birds of West Africa. The arrangement of the birds is essentially the same as that of Bannerman, minor departures having been made to group birds of similar size on the same plate. An attempt has been made to avoid the use of colour adjectives that allude to things that are unfamiliar in West Africa (e.g. chestnut, slate). Technical terms have been kept to a minimum. For reasons of space it has not been possible to include information on the size, colouring and numbers of eggs.

The study of birds is only just beginning in West Africa. There are many gaps to fill in our present knowledge, and probably a good many misconceptions to correct. Up till now nearly all knowledge of animal distribution has depended on the observations of a handful of Europeans, most of whom have been primarily engaged in other work. There can be little further progress until the new generation of educated Africans help to extend knowledge by becoming interested in the animals of their own environment and by keeping accurate records of their observations. It is hoped that this book may help to stimulate such interest in birds, particularly amongst young Africans.

I should like to record my thanks to the staff of Messrs. Longmans, Green & Co. for their kindness and help during the preparation of this book and to my wife who helped with proof-reading and with many suggestions for its contents. Finally, I must thank the artist, Ernest Mansell, for his patience and forbearance during the production of the figures. His contribution to this book is more important than mine.

J. H. E.

University College, Ibadan.

INTRODUCTION

The purpose of this book is to enable you to learn something of the common birds that, because they are relatively fearless of man, you are likely to meet without going far afield. In particular, chiefly through the coloured plates, it aims at helping you to identify and name these birds. Why should we trouble to know the names of the birds? There are two main reasons. Only when we know the exact name of a bird can we find out, from books or by asking others, what is already known about it. Secondly, only when we know the identity of a bird can our own observations help to extend the common pool of knowledge.

Before we start identifying birds we should first appreciate their relationship with other animals, their great variety, and know enough about their structure to be able to describe them accurately. From the zoological point of view birds are described as vertebrate animals (i.e. animals with backbones) belonging to the Class Aves (Latin for birds). The other Classes of Vertebrates are Mammals, Reptiles, Amphibians and Fishes. Invertebrates include a wide variety of animal life including insects, worms, snails and jellyfish.

The birds are first subdivided into two major groups: the *Ratitae* or Running Birds; and the *Carinatae* or Flying Birds. The Ratitae include a very small number of forms, the Ostrich being the only African representative. The further classification of the Carinatae is a very difficult matter, outside the scope of this book. Ornithologists, as bird students are called, do not always agree among themselves over the details. But broadly speaking the form of the beak, adapted to obtaining different kinds of food, and the form of the legs and feet, adapted to different uses such as running, swimming and perching, are regarded as being of paramount importance in classification. Other features of importance include the arrangement of the feathers, the form of the voice apparatus, the structure of the skull and the nesting habits. A recent classification gives 22 *Orders* for the carinate birds of the world, divided into 162 *Families* and comprising nearly 9,000 different distinct kinds or *species*. All but 2 of these orders have West African representatives in 77 families with over 1,000 species. These figures are mentioned to show that West Africa has a very good share of the world's wealth of bird life. It will be appreciated therefore that this book deals only with a fraction of the birds of West Africa, the 100 species being taken from 35 families. A note has been included on each of these families and you will find it contains information applicable to each of the species from that family, so that the family note as well as the species paragraph should be read together.

You will find each species has both an English name and a Latin scientific name. The scientific name is of great value, as it is understood the world over. It consists of two words, e.g. *Milvus migrans*, the name for the Black Kite. The first part is called the *generic* name and the second the *specific* name. There are other kinds of Kite in different parts of the world. All belong to the genus *Milvus*, but are distinct species, *Milvus milvus* being the Red Kite, once a common scavenger in the streets of London, but now a rare bird.

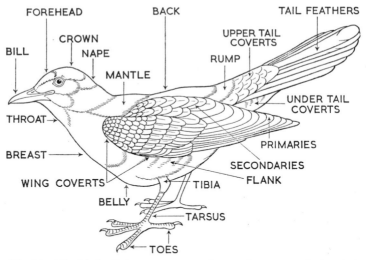

To identify birds it is necessary to know the names for various parts of their external anatomy, as many of these terms have been used in the descriptions that follow. The best way to learn these is by studying the accompanying diagram.

When using this book, since it is small enough to carry with you, it may often be possible to compare the coloured figure with the bird as you actually meet it. You should then turn to the written paragraph and confirm your identification, making sure that the bird is the right size. Size is so important that a scale has been included on each of the plates, and in the text certain terms have been used to describe size. The table below lists these terms together with the actual sizes to which they refer and also an example of a common bird to which the term applies. Thus if you decide that a bird you see is "about the size of a sparrow" it should be described as "small". If it is not, it may well mean that your identification is at fault, though some allowance must be made for the difficulty with border-line cases.

Descriptive Term	Actual size range	Common Example
Tiny	Less than 4 in.	Bronze Mannikin
Small	4 in. to 6 in.	Sparrow
Small medium	6 in. to 8 in.	Village Weaver
Medium	8 in. to 12 in.	Bulbul
Medium large	12 in. to 20 in.	Coucal
Large	20 in. to 30 in.	Pied Crow
Very large	Over 30 in.	Vulture

If you meet a bird not mentioned in this book, or when the book is not with you, try to write down a systematic description of it. Start with the beak, then work over the crown of the head down to the tail. Then describe the wings, the underparts from chin to belly and finish with the legs and feet. The coloured plates have made it unnecessary to describe details of the plumage, so only those more striking points that will help in recognition have been mentioned. In addition reference has been made to other closely similar species with which the one under consideration may be confused, so that you may know what points of detail to observe.

One of the difficulties confronting experienced ornithologists, as well as beginners, is the variation in the plumage of a single species of bird. In many birds the males and females have quite different appearances. In others the young differ markedly from the adults. In a few there are distinct colour varieties and some have distinct breeding and non-breeding (*eclipse*) plumages. In a book of this size it has only been possible to refer to the more outstanding of these points. If there is no mention of sexual differences, it can be assumed that the two sexes are essentially alike.

So far all the emphasis has been on correct recognition of the species. This is because it is the essential starting point for further knowledge. Once the species has been identified something of its distribution, habits and call can be learned from this book. But soon you will know more about some common species in your home area than the space available here can include, so be sure to keep records of your observations. You may easily discover things that are not yet known. In due course you will want to consult larger books to obtain information on species not included here and to get details on topics, such as the size and colouring of eggs, for which no space has been found.

The descriptions which follow are given in note form to save space, and are arranged under four main headings for easy reference in the field.

Note.—On the plates, the symbol ♂ denotes "Male" and the symbol ♀ denotes "Female".

HERONS AND EGRETS

(Ardeidae)

Mainly water-side birds with long legs and necks and a long bill used for catching fish, frogs and insects. In flight the neck is bent so that the head is sunk between the shoulders, the feet extend behind the short tail and the wing beat is slow and deliberate.

1. Cattle Egret

Bubulcus ibis *(Plate I, 1)*

One of Africa's best-known birds, the only white bird seen regularly away from water.

RECOGNITION. Medium large. Plumage appears entirely white at all seasons, though when breeding buff-coloured plumes on crown, back and throat are visible at close range. Bill yellow; legs greenish. The similar Little Egret has black bill and legs.

DISTRIBUTION. Occurs throughout Africa and elsewhere. A regular migrant in West Africa, moving north in the rains to breed, south in the dry season.

HABITS. Cattle Egrets feed, fly and roost in flocks. They feed on insects disturbed by the feet of grazing cattle. They hardly ever perch on the backs of cattle and do not normally feed on ticks. Flocks, flying in V-formation to their roosts, are a familiar evening sight. Roosting usually occurs in large trees, sometimes in busy towns. The species nests in colonies, sometimes with other herons. In West Africa nesting occurs during the rains after the northerly migration.

CALL. Mainly silent though occasionally making a harsh croak. When breeding, however, they chatter incessantly at the nests.

VULTURES

(*Aegypiidae*)

Large repulsive birds with much of the head, sometimes also the neck, devoid of feathers. They have powerful hooked bills and strong claws. Vultures are scavengers, rapidly assembling at a carcass. Differ from true Birds of Prey in the lack of head feathers. The beautiful soaring flight compensates for repulsiveness on the ground.

2. Common or Hooded Vulture   (*Plate I, 2*)

Necrosyrtes monachus

This is the only really common species of vulture in West Africa. Seldom seen far from towns and villages, where it is a valuable scavenger.

RECOGNITION. Very large (though smaller than most vultures). The plumage is mottled dark brown. Facial part of the head, throat and front of neck are devoid of feathers and pink to purple in colour. In soaring flight the rounded tail and separated wing-tip feathers are characters to note.

DISTRIBUTION. Common throughout the savannah of West Africa and has a very interesting sporadic occurrence within the forest zone also.

HABITS. Usually gregarious. When perched in a tree or on a roof top it adopts a characteristic hunched-up pose. Soars on motionless wings in warm uprising air-currents. When a soaring bird discovers food its descent to it is noted by others so that several birds soon collect. It nests in trees during the dry season.

CALL. None known, except for food-begging cries of the young.

FALCONS, KITES, BUZZARDS, EAGLES, etc.

(*Falconidae*)

This family, the true Birds of Prey, can be recognised easily by the powerful hooked bills and strong claws. The different species are difficult to separate because the sexes often differ in size and the young take some years to achieve characteristic adult plumage.

Plate I

1 Cattle Egret   4 Black-shouldered Kite

2 Common or Hooded Vulture   5 Lizard-Buzzard

3 Black Kite

Plate II

INCHES

6	Shikra	9	Red-eyed Turtle-Dove
7	Bush-fowl	10	Laughing Dove
8	Speckled Pigeon		

3. Black Kite (*Plate I, 3*)

Milvus migrans

The best-known of all African birds of prey, seen chiefly near towns and villages.

RECOGNITION. Large. Plumage entirely shades of dark brown. The forked tail is distinctive. Adults have a yellow bill. The forked tail and long pointed wings make an unmistakable flight silhouette.

DISTRIBUTION. Different races occur throughout Africa and all are somewhat migratory. The West African race seems to move northward in the rains and southward to breed in the dry season.

HABITS. Seen singly or in large parties. Kites are mainly scavengers, often met in early morning cleaning the night's kill from roads. River and harbour offal and the victims of bush fires also afford food. Sometimes catch insects (e.g. Termites) in their claws while flying. They have an easy flapping flight, but also soar in rising air particularly at bush fires. Numbers roost year after year in a favoured tree. Nests are built in high trees in the dry season.

CALL. A drawn-out and plaintive "Peeeeee-yewrrrr", heard specially at midday.

4. Black-shouldered Kite (*Plate I, 4*)

Elanus caeruleus

More a bird of open country than the Black Kite but is often seen in gardens.

RECOGNITION. Medium large. Pale grey above except for black feathers on the shoulders. The face and underparts pure white. A few black feathers through the eye give a "Chinese" appearance.

DISTRIBUTION. Resident throughout Africa and fairly common generally in our area.

HABITS. Solitary or in pairs. In addition to its distinctive plumage it has three conspicuous habits. In flight it pauses with wings lifted above the back in a shallow "V". Secondly it is quite the most likely hawk to be seen hovering, appearing to stand on its tail in the air, with rapidly beating wings. Thirdly after alighting on the top of a tree it raises and depresses its tail vigorously. Feeds on lizards, mice, small birds and insects. Nests in tall trees over a considerable part of the year but relatively little is known on this subject.

CALL. Silent except when breeding. The young squeak to attract attention and parents warn with harsh screams.

5. Lizard-Buzzard   *(Plate I, 5)*

Kaupifalco monogrammicus

A widespread and fairly common hawk that is quite distinct in appearance and voice.

RECOGNITION. Medium large. The entire upperparts a uniform grey, the throat white with a central black streak, the remaining underparts finely barred black and white. Conspicuous white bars cross the mostly black tail.

DISTRIBUTION. Resident throughout West Africa and most of the rest of the continent in both forest and savannah country.

HABITS. Usually seen singly perching within the foliage of a tree. It feeds chiefly on lizards, insects, toads and mice, rarely on small birds. The flight consists of alternate periods of rapidly beating wings and glidings and finishes with an upward swoop with spread tail into a tree, displaying the tail pattern. The nest is placed in a tree-fork at some height from the ground; the breeding period is usually just before the rains.

CALL. A loud ringing whistle of "ta-lee-yu-lu-lu-lu-lu" that is unmistakable once learned.

6. Shikra   *(Plate II, 6)*

Accipiter badius

Probably the commonest and most widely distributed of the smaller birds of prey.

RECOGNITION. Female medium large and male medium. The upperparts and head are grey; the underparts and underside of the wing are finely barred with reddish-brown. It appears a small pale-coloured hawk with rounded wings when seen flying overhead.

4

DISTRIBUTION. Occurs throughout West Africa and also most of Africa south of the Sahara, specially common in wooded savannah.

HABITS. Solitary or in pairs. A very active little hawk feeding on lizards and small birds. It perches within the foliage of a tree and then dashes out after prey, seizes it in its claws and swoops up into a tree again to devour its victim. It very frequently takes lizards off house walls, sometimes from within the shelter of a verandah. It draws attention by being noisy at times especially in the breeding season. The nest is built in a tree usually towards the end of the dry season.

CALL. Two chief calls are heard. One is a rapid high-pitched "Kwee, Kwee, Kwee, Kwee" and the other "K'wick, K'wick, K'wick".

GAME BIRDS

(Family Phasianidae)

Mainly ground birds with powerful feet and claws used in scratching for food. The hind toe is raised above the level of the front toes. Many kinds, like the Francolins, both sexes possess a mottled brownish plumage that conceals them well, but others have drab females while the males are elaborately coloured, as in the Peacock.

7. Bush-fowl   (Plate II, 7)

Francolinus bicalcaratus

There are about a dozen different kinds of francolin in West Africa but this species is the only one that could be called common or widespread.

RECOGNITION. Medium large. The plumage appears brownish but close inspection reveals a beautiful patterning of the feathers, those of the underparts having markings that are distinctive for this species. There are usually two spurs above the hind toe of old males.

DISTRIBUTION. Throughout West Africa except in thickly forested parts.

HABITS. These ground birds spend most of their time moving in small parties through grass, farms and the like in search of food. If disturbed they take to the wing with a whirring low flight, often

5

calling hoarsely at the same time. But they tend to keep concealed on the ground unless disturbed. No real nest is made, the five or six eggs being laid in a natural hollow on the ground. Breeding occurs at the beginning of the dry season.

CALL. A most unmusical croaking call of "Quairk" heard chiefly at dusk and dawn.

PIGEONS

(*Family Columbidae*)

Pigeons are stocky fast-flying birds, mostly feeding on the ground, though one group feed on ripe fruits in the tree tops. All pigeons build loose nests of sticks, through which the white eggs can be seen.

8. Speckled Pigeon (*Plate II, 8*)

Columba guinea

One of the largest pigeons of West Africa, this species is readily distinguished from other members of the family by size and conspicuous colouring.

RECOGNITION. Medium large. The plumage is grey on the head, back and underparts, and mainly a rich purple-brown on the upper back and wings. The wings have conspicuous whitish markings, giving rise to the English name. The eye has bright-red bare skin round it. The grey of the lower back appears almost white when the bird is in flight.

DISTRIBUTION. Throughout the savannah of West Africa and through to East Africa.

HABITS. Often feeds in flocks on the ground in early morning and late afternoon. When not feeding they often perch on house roofs and draw attention by their calling. In the hottest hours shelter in trees, especially the Borassus palm. Nesting occurs mainly in the first quarter of the year.

CALL. A deep and repeated "Kroo-roo-roo-roo".

9. Red-eyed Turtle-Dove *(Plate II, 9)*

Streptopelia semitorquata

A good-sized pigeon rather similar to several closely related species, though the most common and widely spread of them.

RECOGNITION. Medium large. This pigeon and its close relatives can be distinguished from all other pigeons by a half collar of black feathers round the back of the neck. Good size, general dark-brown plumage and the absence of any white in the tail distinguishes this particular dove. Its call-note is the best distinction.

DISTRIBUTION. Throughout West Africa but in the northern parts it is mainly confined to river valleys.

HABITS. Solitary or in groups. Often perch on tree-tops to call. From this perch the male will ascend with loud clapping flight and glide down again with down-curved wings in display. It is fond of water and in the driest months tends only to be found near water. It feeds on a variety of foods on the ground, notably ground nuts and peppers. The breeding season is long but nests are found chiefly in the dry season near water.

CALL. A very characteristic "coo, KOO, coo, coo, coo, coo" and a mewing call when the bird alights.

10. Laughing Dove *(Plate II, 10)*

Stigmatopelia senegalensis

This small dove shows a liking for towns and villages and can therefore claim to be the best known of the pigeon family.

RECOGNITION. Medium size. The wings have margins of blue-grey, the rest of the upperparts and breast a purplish-brown but the belly white. The outer tail feathers mainly white, showing clearly in flight. At the base of the throat there is a "bib" of black-edged feathers.

DISTRIBUTION. Occurs throughout Africa south of the Sahara, but in forest country occurs only in clearings.

HABITS. Usually two or more together. A very tame species, feeding on the ground in compounds, town streets, farms and on cassava grinding rocks. It seems to be dependent on man's activities

7

for its food. It seldom flies far and on rising from the ground the wings are clapped together noisily. Nests have been found in every month, but the early rains seems the most active time.

CALL. A monotonously repeated "oo-too-too-TOO-too".

11. Red-billed Wood-Dove (*Plate III, 11*)

Turtur afer

The two Wood-Doves, this species and the Black-billed, are very similar to each other, but easily distinguished from all other pigeons.

RECOGNITION. Medium size. The head bluish-grey, the upperparts earth brown, but with dark-blue spots on the wings, the underparts pink-brown. In flight the predominant colour is bright reddish-brown on the wings, and black bars show across the rump. The pink bill and voice distinguish this species from the Black-billed.

DISTRIBUTION. Throughout the southern parts of West Africa, but replaced by the Black-billed Wood-Dove, farther north, though the two overlap.

HABITS. Solitary or in pairs. Feeds on the ground, particularly cultivated ground. In late afternoon is often seen on road margins. The rather monotonous call is heard chiefly in the heat of the day in the dry season and is usually made while the bird is concealed within a low tree. Breeding occurs mostly in the dry season, nests often being placed quite low.

CALL. A long, "Coo—coo—coo—coo—coo, coo, coo, coo, coo", the notes becoming faster.

12. Green Fruit-Pigeon (*Plate III, 12*)

Treron australis

There are two kinds of Green Pigeons in West Africa. They stand apart from other pigeons in habits as well as colouring.

RECOGNITION. Medium size. The plumage appears mainly green, though a close view reveals several shades of this colour, some purple on the wing and bright yellow on the legs and belly. The best way to distinguish this species from the other green pigeon (*T. waalia*) is by a patch of bright-red bare skin at the base of the bill.

DISTRIBUTION. Throughout West Africa in forest and tree savannah, the other species being more northerly.

HABITS. Sometimes flies, and often feeds, in small flocks. A very fast flier. A bird of the trees, it feeds mainly on fruits, especially on wild figs. It so well matches the foliage that it is very difficult to see. Breeding occurs through most of the year.

CALL. Quite unlike the typical "cooing" of pigeons. A long drawn-out "Kioo-ioo——Kioo-ioo——turrrr-turrrr-yioo".

OWLS

(*Strigidae*)

Owls are nocturnal birds of prey with hooked beak and powerful claws, associated with raptorial habits. They are noted also for silent flight and binocular vision, the large eyes being set looking forward in a rounded "face".

13. White-faced Owl   (*Plate III, 13*)

Ptilopsis leucotis

One of the commonest and most widespread of West African owls, heard calling at night, and not infrequently captured.

RECOGNITION. Medium size. The plumage is mainly brown and grey, much darker on the upper surface and streaky below. The greyish-white facial region is margined with black feathers. Above the eyes are two tufts of feathers that can be erected to stand well up; they are miscalled "ear tufts". The large eye has a bright-yellow iris.

DISTRIBUTION. Throughout West Africa, north of the forest belt.

HABITS. Hides by day in thick foliage but may be seen flying out in the dusk, when there may be enough light to see its chief features. Its presence is announced by the characteristic monotonous call, made throughout the hours of darkness. Feeds on insects, mice, etc. It normally breeds in a tree hollow, laying two white eggs in a nest of sticks.

CALL. The male makes a two-note call of "Kuk-coooo".

9

PLANTAIN-EATERS AND TOURACOS

(*Musophagidae*)

A family of good-sized and usually strikingly coloured birds not found outside Africa. They are mainly fruit-eaters with powerful arched bills and long tails.

14. Grey Plantain-eater   (*Plate III, 14*)

Crinifer piscator

The only dull-coloured member of the family in West Africa but by far the best-known as the others are shy birds mostly from forest country.

RECOGNITION. Medium large with long tail. Upperparts grey-brown, throat and breast brown, the rest of the underparts white with many dark streaks. There is a short crest on the back of the head and the bill is yellow. In flight a white patch is conspicuous in the nearly black wings.

DISTRIBUTION. In savannah country throughout West Africa though rather less common east of the Niger.

HABITS. Usually seen in pairs or small parties keeping mainly in the tree-tops. They can run along branches and usually fly in single file. They feed on a variety of vegetable foods, fruits, seeds, flowers and even leaves. A noisy species with a wide range of calls. Substantial nests of sticks are built in high trees, usually during the drier months.

CALL. The most characteristic are "Cow, cow, cow" and "Charr-titi-charr".

CUCKOOS AND COUCALS

(*Cuculidae*)

Cuckoos are parasitic, laying their eggs in the nests of other birds. Coucals make their own nests. Both groups feed mainly on insects, especially caterpillars. They have loud voices making easily recognised calls.

15. Levaillant's Cuckoo (Plate III, 15)

Clamator levaillantii

Representative of the larger cuckoos as the next species is of the smaller ones.

RECOGNITION. Medium size with long tail. The upperparts black and underparts white but with black streaks on the throat. A short crest on the head. A white bar in the wing and white tips to the feathers of the long graduated tail are also conspicuous.

DISTRIBUTION. Throughout most of Africa south of the Sahara but subject to migratory movements.

HABITS. This species, usually solitary, tends to remain in cover, but reveals its presence by the loud ringing call. It is conspicuous enough when caught flying in the open with rapid wing beats. Certainly migratory in the drier parts of West Africa, there is still much to learn of its movements. It usually deposits its eggs in the nests of different species of Babbler.

CALL. In two phases: the first a slow melancholy "Ki-er, ki-er, ki-er", the second a loud laughing cry of "Kwi, kwi, kwi", in rapid time.

16. Didric Cuckoo (Plate IV, 16)

Lampromorpha caprius

Can be confused with Klaas' cuckoo in appearance, though its call is distinctive. It is West Africa's commonest cuckoo.

RECOGNITION. Small. The male is metallic green above and white below, the female rather more brown above. Both have white spots in wings and tail. Klaas' cuckoo has white outer tail feathers and other minor differences.

DISTRIBUTION. Throughout Africa south of the Sahara apart from the unfarmed forest.

HABITS. Solitary or in pairs. A conspicuous little bird chiefly on account of its loud clear call, usually made from a favourite perch, though also in flight. A large number of small birds have acted as host to the young of this cuckoo but most are different kinds of weavers, especially the Village Weaver. It is subject to some migratory movement.

CALL. A plaintive and repeated "Di-di-di-deea-deea".

17. Senegal Coucal   *(Plate IV, 17)*

Centropus senegalensis

This common coucal exists in two colour varieties, normal and dark. The former can be confused with the rarer Blue-headed Coucal.

RECOGNITION. Medium large with long tail. The normal bird has black crown (not deep blue), black tail, red-brown back and wings and is pure to buffish-white below. The dark variety has black head and throat, most other parts red-brown.

DISTRIBUTION. The normal type is found throughout West Africa, except high forest; the dark type is known only from Ghana to southern Nigeria.

HABITS. Solitary, in pairs or small parties. A rather skulking bird, more often heard than seen. Clumsy in flight it seems to lose its balance when alighting. It has a curious habit of extending one wing and remaining poised, then darting forward to catch an insect on the ground. The species builds a large domed nest of grass near to the ground. The two varieties interbreed.

CALL. A variety of notes, the most characteristic call is a descending "Coo-coo-coo-coo-coo", suggesting water poured from a bottle.

NIGHTJARS

(Caprimulgidae)

Nightjars are nocturnal birds with plumages of mottled browns, greys and blacks effectively concealing them by day, whether on the ground or lying lengthwise on a tree branch. By night they fly round feeding on insects, are noted for their "churring" calls, and often rest on roads, especially dirt ones.

18. Long-tailed Nightjar   *(Plate IV, 18)*

Scotornis climacurus

Selected to represent the family because it is both common and relatively easy to identify, chiefly seen when moving at night with a light, such as by car or bicycle.

RECOGNITION. Small bird with long tail. Plumage grey-brown streaked with black. The distinctive features of this species are con-

12

spicuous white patches in the wing and a long graduated tail. The eye shines red in the dark when picked up by a car's lights.

DISTRIBUTION. Throughout West Africa but subject to migratory movement, entering the forest area only in the dry season.

HABITS. Usually concealed on the ground by day it emerges at dusk with silent flight to catch insects. When settled on a road at night it can be approached quite closely before taking off. Two eggs are laid on the bare ground, after the northward migration.

CALL. A loud "churrrrr" that may be sustained almost without break throughout the night, especially during moonlight.

SWIFTS

(*Micropodidae*)

Swifts are small birds remarkable for rapid flight on long, narrow, curved wings. They have short wide bills adapted to catch insects while in flight. The weak feet are only used to cling to trees, rocks or buildings where swifts nest and roost. Most of the day is spent in active flight; the ground is never visited.

19. Little African Swift (*Plate IV, 19*)

Colletoptera affinis

Essentially a town bird and must therefore be known to all.

RECOGNITION. Small. The long, curved wings, typical of swifts will first be noticed. It is distinguished from other swifts by having both a square-cut tail (not forked) and a white rump, most of the rest of the plumage being black.

DISTRIBUTION. Common throughout West Africa but subject to some local migration.

HABITS. Most often seen in noisy parties, often numbered in hundreds, wheeling over the house-tops of towns and villages during the prolonged breeding season. They are rather more dispersed during the driest months. Nests, often many together, are made under bridges and among house rafters; mud, feathers and grass being used in their construction. Two long white eggs are usual.

CALL. Rather like other swifts, a shrill, harsh "creeeeee".

20. Palm Swift *(Plate IV, 20)*

Cypsiurus parvus

A very common and widespread swift, distinguished by smaller size and relatively longer tail from the migrant European Swift.

RECOGNITION. Small. The wings are exceptionally slender and curved. The whole plumage is grey-brown; savannah birds being greyer, those from the forest zone more brown. The tail is long, slender and forked: when flying straight the two prongs are held together, but are separated as the bird turns.

DISTRIBUTION. Throughout West Africa and beyond.

HABITS. Usually in flocks. Always associated with palms, at least for nesting; coconut and oil-palms in the south, Borassus palms in the north. While parties circle in feeding flight individuals may drop out to cling beneath a palm frond till the group returns. Nests are J-shaped in section, the vertical cemented beneath a palm frond and the curve the nest-cup. The breeding season is not sharply defined.

CALL. A very shrill screaming call.

ROLLERS

(*Coraciidae*)

Rollers are good-sized, brightly coloured birds. Their name is derived from their remarkable powers of flight; which includes an ability to roll over sideways. Rollers feed on insects and are bold and conspicuous birds. All nest in tree holes, laying pure white eggs.

21. Abyssinian or Senegal Roller *(Plate V, 21)*

Coracias abyssinica

Many consider this West Africa's most beautiful bird.

RECOGNITION. Medium size with very long tail. Although the back is brown the rest of the plumage is mainly blue and the bird usually appears entirely blue except at close range. The tail has very elongated outer feathers that distinguish it from the migrant European Roller. A powerful black bill.

DISTRIBUTION. Throughout the drier northern parts of West Africa, where it is common though partially migratory.

HABITS. Usually solitary. Conspicuous, not only by colouring, but also by perching on telegraph wires and low bare trees, from which it swoops down to catch insects on the ground. It is aggressive towards intruding birds irrespective of size, chasing them off with harsh cries. It is attracted by grass fires. Breeding occurs in the early rains.

CALL. A variety of harsh screechings, notably "Kreek, kreek, kreek".

22. Broad-billed Roller   (*Plate V, 22*)

Eurystomus afer

A noisy handsome bird that is bound to attract attention. Can only be confused with the Blue-throated roller.

RECOGNITION. Medium size. Appears, when perched, to be purplish-brown in colour with large bright-yellow bill. In flight the presence of bright-blue feathers in wings and tail is revealed. Blue under the tail and violet-washed underparts are seen at close range. Absence of a blue throat distinguishes it from the Blue-throated species.

DISTRIBUTION. Throughout those parts of West Africa with good-sized trees but also locally migrant.

HABITS. Solitary or in pairs, sometimes flocking. Draws attention by harsh cries and by perching conspicuously. During the whole period of breeding activity it is a most aggressive bird driving off Kites and Crows with noisy swooping attacks. Large numbers of birds will congregate at a termite flight. The species becomes active in the last light, flying silently over the trees before roosting. Breeding occurs at the end of the dry season.

CALL. A variety of harsh calls. Characteristic are "Schar-a-roc" and "Yarrr".

WOOD-HOOPOES

(*Phoeniculidae*)

A family of long-tailed, medium-sized birds, with long, curved bills. They are mostly noisy birds that cling with sharp claws to the sides of trees in search of insects.

23. Guinea Wood-Hoopoe or Kakelaar (*Plate V, 23*)

Phoeniculus erythrorhynchos

The only common member of the family and a particularly noisy species.

RECOGNITION. Medium size with long tail. The plumage is a glossy blue-black relieved by white in the wings and tail that only shows clearly in flight. The exceptionally long and graduated tail has all but the middle feathers with white near the tip. The long, curved bill and feet are bright red. (Young birds have a black bill.)

DISTRIBUTION. Common and widespread in Nigeria, less so in Ghana and apparently unknown west of the Ivory Coast.

HABITS. Most often seen in small parties, the birds fly from tree to tree in single file calling softly. When assembled they become noisy, bobbing up and down and flirting their tails. The tree is then searched for insects, birds run along the boughs, move jerkily clinging to the trunk and may drop to the ground. Little is known of breeding habits, except that pale-blue eggs are laid in tree holes.

CALL. A sharp call of "Aq" but repeated so rapidly, when excited, as to sound like a rattle.

HORNBILLS

(*Bucerotidae*)

Mostly fairly large birds with enormous bills often with a raised "casque". The breeding habits of the family, still imperfectly known, are most remarkable. The female is walled up in a tree hollow while incubating; only a small hole being left through which the male feeds her.

24. Grey Hornbill (*Plate V, 24*)

Lophoceros nasutus

The common savannah hornbill, but somewhat like the Red-beaked Hornbill from farther north.

RECOGNITION. Medium large with long tail. Plumage mainly grey and brown but with paler underparts. A little white in the wings and

16

tips of the outer tail feathers. The bill is mainly black in the male, red-tipped in the female. (The Red-beaked Hornbill has much more white in the plumage and a red bill.)

DISTRIBUTION. Widespread in savannah throughout West Africa, extending nearly to the desert, where it meets the Red-beaked Hornbill.

HABITS. Often seen in small parties. The flight is very characteristic, consisting of alternate short flapping climbs and downward glides. Insects as well as fruits are eaten. Has a habit of perching on top of a tree, stretching up the neck and uttering the mournful long-carrying cry. Subject to some imperfectly understood local migrations. Breeding in tree holes, like all Hornbills, towards the end of the dry season.

CALL. A loud prolonged very plaintive "Pee-ye".

25. Allied Hornbill (*Plate V, 25*)

Lophoceros semifasciatus

The name is unfortunate but indicates relationship with a species occurring outside West Africa.

RECOGNITION. Medium large with long tail. Plumage black and white, the white being confined to the underside from breast to tail base, and to white tips to two lateral tail feathers on each side. The wholly black wing distinguishes it from most other hornbills. Massive pale-yellow bill, black at the tip.

DISTRIBUTION. Throughout the forests of West Africa and extending well into the savannah along rivers and streams.

HABITS. Somewhat gregarious, flocks of a score are not uncommon. Feeds on fruits and insects in tree-tops morning and evening, but comes lower down in the heat of the day. An ungainly flapping flight but also glides gracefully. When calling will become very excited, the head being stretched up and the whole bird rocks with the effort. Beyond the fact that it conforms to the family habits, little else is known of its nesting.

CALL. A loud, continued, rapid whistle of "Pi, pi, pi——pi, pi, pi——pi, pi, pi".

17

KINGFISHERS

(*Alcedinidae*)

Kingfishers are mostly brightly coloured birds, vivid blue being characteristic. Long, straight bills for fish-catching are typical, though many have abandoned fish in favour of insects as staple diet. The legs are disproportionately weak. Kingfishers nest in holes, usually in trees or river banks, and lay rounded white eggs.

26. Pigmy Kingfisher   (*Plate VI, 26*)

Ispidina picta

A beautiful tiny bird, usually met away from water. Another similar Kingfisher, the Malachite, is met over water.

RECOGNITION. Tiny size. Upperparts vivid blue, underparts orange red. Throat, and a spot on the side of the neck, white; sides of the head washed with purple. The bill and feet are bright red. There is no crest to the head. (The Malachite Kingfisher has a crested head and lacks the purplish facial area.)

DISTRIBUTION. Throughout West Africa and beyond; less common in the north.

HABITS. Usually in pairs, sometimes solitary. The flight is rapid, darting and of short duration. Although an insect-eating species it enjoys a bath, diving into the surface of a puddle repeatedly. Has a curious habit of jerkily raising and lowering the head. During display the head is inclined so that beak and backbone are in line and the short tail is raised. Usually nests in holes in banks that the bird excavates for itself.

CALL. A shrill piping call, not very loud, of "pee-pee-pee".

27. Senegal Kingfisher   (*Plate VI, 27*)

Halcyon senegalensis

The commonest of three rather similar Kingfishers, it is one of West Africa's most conspicuous birds. The other two species are the Blue-breasted (No. 28) and the Red-bellied Kingfishers.

Plate III

INCHES

11 Red-billed Wood-Dove	14 Grey Plantain-eater
12 Green Fruit-Pigeon	15 Levaillant's Cuckoo
13 White-faced Owl	

Plate IV

16 Didric Cuckoo

17 Senegal Coucal

18 Long-tailed Nightjar

19 Little African Swift

20 Palm Swift

RECOGNITION. Small medium. Head **grey, back and tail light** blue, wings deeper blue and black. The underparts are uniform pale grey, distinguishing this from the two similar species. Bill with red upper mandible and black lower one. Feet black.

DISTRIBUTION. Throughout most of Africa south of the Sahara, subject to local migration.

HABITS. Seen singly or in pairs. A mainly insectivorous species, it perches watching for ground insects, then dives down to secure them. Favourite perches, employed day after day, may be a tree bough or a telegraph wire. The flight is low, swift and usually of short duration. It prefers damp places in the dry season. When breeding, pairs display by standing erect facing each other, opening and closing the wings. Nests mostly in tree holes during the early rains, when it becomes noisy.

CALL. A rising and falling rattle; also an incessant "Yimp, tirr-r-r-r-r-r" in the breeding season.

28. Blue-breasted Kingfisher (*Plate VI, 28*)

Halcyon malimbicus

More shy than the last species but by no means uncommon.

RECOGNITION. Medium size. Crown grey, back and tail light-blue, wings blue and black. Most of underside is pale grey but the breast is sky blue, distinguishing this species. Bill with red upper and black lower mandibles. Feet red.

DISTRIBUTION. Throughout the wooded parts of West Africa; well into savannah country near rivers and streams.

HABITS. Usually solitary. Shy, in the sense that it keeps largely in shelter, nevertheless comes into gardens and reveals its presence with loud calling. Insectivorous, but said also to catch fish; it certainly frequents streams. Nests in tree holes or excavates a hole in an old termite nest.

CALL. A loud alarm call of "chack". The breeding season "song" a much repeated "Cheu-che, che, che, cheu-cheu".

29. Striped Kingfisher (*Plate VI, 29*)

Halcyon chelicuti

Smaller, and more dull-coloured than the last two species, it is nevertheless obviously a kingfisher.

RECOGNITION. Small. The bill shape proclaims a kingfisher, and in flight bright blue on the back, rump and open wing becomes apparent. At rest the upperparts and closed wings appear streaky brown and the underparts whitish with dark streaks, the "kingfisher blue" being almost hidden. Bill: upper mandible dark brown, lower red. Feet dull red.

DISTRIBUTION. Widespread in savannah country throughout Africa; sometimes in forest farms.

HABITS. Usually seen singly, it will perch conspicuously watching for insect food. A quick darting flight, used aggressively against intruders. Display behaviour, with opening and shutting of wings, is like that of the Senegal Kingfisher. It breeds early in the rainy season, usually in holes, but has been known to displace swallows from their mud nest under a house roof.

CALL. Usually a slow melancholy "che-heeee" but accelerated in display to a rapid "che, he——che, he——che, he", the wings being opened at each call.

BEE-EATERS

(*Meropidae*)

A family of brilliantly coloured birds with long, slender, slightly down-curving bills. Some species have the centre tail feathers much longer than the rest. All have a sailing flight that shows off the pointed wings. They are mostly migratory, nesting colonially in holes in banks.

30. White-throated Bee-eater (*Plate VI, 30*)

Aerops albicollis

Less brilliant than most bee-eaters, this is the commonest species, with very attractive behaviour.

RECOGNITION Small medium with long tail. At rest appears blue-green above and white below. Black nape, eye stripe and throat collar, the rest of the head white. This black and white head pattern distinguishes it from other greenish bee-eaters. The open wing shows golden-brown. Adult birds have very long centre tail feathers. Curved black bill.

DISTRIBUTION. Breeds in the northern half of West Africa during the rains and migrates south to the coast from October to May.

HABITS. Strongly gregarious, flocks of over a hundred are commonly seen, especially in the evening. Insects, not only bees, are watched for from a conspicuous perch and taken on the wing. Their perch may be low or quite high. The flight is a mixture of flapping and delightfully graceful sailing, usually accompanied by calling. Little is known of the breeding but it occurs in colonies on the fringe of the Sahara.

CALL. A musical twittering made chiefly in flight.

BARBETS

(Capitonidae)

Most barbets are brightly coloured birds having a sturdy appearance and heavy bills for excavating their nests in trees and banks. The short tail, unlike that of woodpeckers, is not used to support the bird. Strong feet alone are used to enable the bird to cling and climb.

31. Tooth-billed Barbet   (Plate VII, 31)

Pogonornis bidentatus

A conspicuously-coloured bird, it is one of the largest barbets of West Africa.

RECOGNITION. Medium size. The upperparts and wings blue-black, except for the lower back which is white (a conspicuous feature in flight). The underparts are dull crimson-red from throat to belly and this distinguishes it from the related savannah species, the Bearded Barbet, which has a wide black band across the breast. White flanks. A patch of bare yellow skin round the eye and a massive, toothed, yellowish bill.

DISTRIBUTION. Throughout wooded West Africa, particularly farms and gardens in forest country.

HABITS. Usually solitary, but small parties sometimes meet. Feeds mainly on fruits especially figs. The flight is heavy, direct, and of short duration. Often remains stationary or nearly so, for a long time. Nests in holes in trees, excavated by the bird usually at a height of 30 feet or more from the ground. Breeding occurs before the rains. Little else known of behaviour and breeding habits.

CALL. Mainly a silent species but has some low guttural calls such as "Kroo-oo".

32. Yellow-fronted Tinker-bird   (*Plate VII, 32*)

Pogoniulus chrysoconus

Tinker-birds are diminutive barbets taking their name from their ringing calls, sounding like beating on metal with a small hammer.

RECOGNITION. Tiny. All tinker-birds are streaky or bluish-black above, yellow below and have white stripes on the head. This species is easily distinguished by a golden-yellow patch on the forehead, and by having its upperparts much streaked with white. Its call too is distinctive.

DISTRIBUTION. Widespread and common in the savannah of West Africa.

HABITS. Usually solitary. Much time is spent calling, otherwise it searches trees for insects. When calling will remain in one place for long periods. When feeding it appears very alert and searches each branch thoroughly. The flight is weak and undulating, usually to the next tree. Nesting holes are made in tree stumps, often quite low, during the rainy season.

CALL. A monotonous repetition of "tonk-tonk-tonk", the notes spaced out uniformly at about second intervals, often lasting several minutes.

WOODPECKERS

(*Picidae*)

Woodpeckers not only excavate nesting holes in trees, they also feed largely on such wood-boring insects as beetle larvae. For this life they have a long stout bill, a very long sticky tongue, strong feet and a tail with stiff feathers to help support the bird while clinging to a vertical tree trunk.

33. Grey Woodpecker   (*Plate VII, 33*)

Mesopicos goertae

This is not only a common woodpecker, it is more easily distinguished than most.

RECOGNITION. Small medium. The head and underside are grey though the male has a crimson crown. The back and wings are greenish, the rump is bright red though this is almost hidden when the bird is still. The stiff tail feathers are nearly black. Bill, long and sharp.

DISTRIBUTION. Races of this bird occur throughout the savannah of Africa.

HABITS. Typical woodpeckers all have much the same habits. Usually not more than two birds together. They feed on insects obtained from bark crevices or from boring into rotting wood. Ants are sometimes taken on the ground. The flight is strong and undulating, and makes a characteristic sound. Mostly silent but becoming noisy in the breeding season. Breeds in the dry season, sometimes in quite low tree stumps.

CALL. A loud "Creee-creee-creee".

LARKS
(*Alaudidae*)

Larks are small birds possessing a dull-brownish plumage. Many soar in the air to sing but otherwise spend their time on the ground, where their colour pattern helps to conceal them. A long curved claw to the hind toe is characteristic.

34. Buckley's Bush-Lark (*Plate VII, 34*)
Mirafra buckleyi

Draws attention to itself by "drumming" its wings in flight.

RECOGNITION. Small. Streaky pinkish-brown above and reddish-buff below with brown spots on the breast. The absence of a crest is noteworthy and the tail has blackish feathers toward each side; marginal and central feathers being reddish-brown. The "drumming" is the best guide to recognition.

DISTRIBUTION. Common in savannah throughout West Africa.

HABITS. A solitary species. Mainly insect-feeding. Its drumming flight is most peculiar and seems to replace song. The bird climbs to some height in a series of loops making the drumming sound with each ascent. Then dives to the ground perhaps also drumming. This habit occurs throughout the year. Breeding occurs in the rains, well concealed nests are made on the ground against a grass tussock.

CALL. Not recorded, but the wing-drumming sounds like "Prrrrp-prrrrp".

35. Crested Lark (*Plate VII, 35*)
Galerida cristata

The best-known lark of West Africa, and very typical of its family.

RECOGNITION. Small medium. Sandy-brown above and with a prominent crest to the head, the feathers curving upwards. Nearly white underparts with dark streaks on the breast.

DISTRIBUTION. Different races occur throughout the drier parts of West Africa.

HABITS. Solitary or in pairs, frequenting open ground such as gardens, farms and roadsides. Tame enough to permit a close approach. Feed on a variety of insects and small seeds. Unlike some other larks they seldom soar, and sing mainly on the ground. Breeding occurs in the dry season, the nest being placed on the ground in a grass tussock.

CALL. A pleasant "trilling" song, particularly in the breeding season.

WAGTAILS, PIPITS AND LONG-CLAWS
(*Motacillidae*)

Essentially ground birds and mainly insectivorous. Wagtails are graceful birds with long tails that are continually moving up and down as the birds run swiftly after food. Pipits and Long-Claws are more robust but also show tail wagging to some extent.

36. African Pied Wagtail (*Plate VIII, 36*)

Motacilla aguimp

Perhaps the most graceful bird in West Africa and certainly one of the tamest.

RECOGNITION. Small. Head, body, wings and tail, all show black and white. A white eyebrow is conspicuous on the black head and a black breast patch contrasts with the white underparts. The black back distinguishes it from other wagtails, though young birds have grey backs. Behaviour distinguishes it from all other black and white birds.

DISTRIBUTION. Widespread in West Africa, but not in very dry country and not extending west of Sierra Leone.

HABITS. Often in small parties. Its quick darting flight, with incessant bobbing movements of the tail when on the ground, make it unmistakable. Very often seen on roadsides, near streams and on house-roofs. Insects are taken low in the air as well as on the ground. Nests are made in banks and against buildings in the early rains.

CALL. A call of "Chizzic" and a sweet musical song of high-pitched notes.

37. Yellow Wagtail (*Plate VIII, 37*)

Budytes flavus

Probably the most numerous migrant from Europe, to be seen in all kinds of open ground that is not too arid.

RECOGNITION. Small. A slender bird with greenish upperparts and yellowish underparts. The birds, especially the young, are rather drab on arrival but the males become very handsome before departure, having a greyish head with conspicuous white eye-brow. The tail-bobbing of wagtails is a valuable guide to identity. Several, slightly different, races occur.

DISTRIBUTION. Breeding in Europe, this species is found throughout West Africa from October to April, particularly in the south.

HABITS. Strongly gregarious, flocks of a hundred are commonly seen, chiefly on closely cut grass but also in farms. When feeding the birds walk forward, all members of the flock tending to face the same way, and then a quick darting pounce is made on some small ground insect. As the time for departure approaches much time is spent preening while perching in trees or bushes and also on short flights. Breeding does not concern us.

CALL. A sharp call of "Chizzit" made chiefly in flight.

38. Plain-backed Pipit (*Plate VIII, 38*)

Anthus leucophrys

Several pipits occur in West Africa that are all rather alike. This species is the most likely to be met, being widespread and fairly common.

RECOGNITION. Small. Like most pipits, earth brown above and nearly white below. The distinguishing features of this species are the absence of streaky patterning on the back and the presence of pronounced dark streaks on the breast. A pale eyebrow and pale (not white) outer tail feathers are also noteworthy.

DISTRIBUTION. Throughout West Africa in forest clearings and all types of savannah.

HABITS. Usually seen in pairs, sometimes in small groups. Essentially ground birds that seldom fly far. They feed chiefly on insects. The tail bobs up and down as the bird walks, like that of a wagtail,

26

Plate V

21 Abyssinian or Senegal Roller   23 Guinea Wood-Hoopoe or Kakelaar
22 Broad-billed Roller   24 Grey Hornbill
                                      25 Allied Hornbill

Plate VI

INCHES

26 Pigmy Kingfisher   29 Striped Kingfisher
27 Senegal Kingfisher   30 White-throated Bee-eater
28 Blue-breasted Kingfisher

Plate VII

INCHES

31   Tooth-billed Barbet

32   Yellow-fronted Tinker-bird

33   Grey Woodpecker

34   Buckley's Bush-Lark

35   Crested Lark

Plate VIII

36	African Pied Wagtail	39	Yellow-throated Long-Claw
37	Yellow Wagtail	40	Brown Babbler
38	Plain-backed Pipit		

though in slower time. Farm land and playing fields are favourite haunts. Nests are built on the ground in the dry season, usually against a grass tuft or on a bank.

CALL. A rather weak call of "tsip", but in the breeding season a song of warbling and chirping notes as well.

39. Yellow-throated Long-Claw (Plate VIII, 39)

Macronyx croceus

The only West African Long-Claw and quite unmistakable.

RECOGNITION. Small medium. Upperparts, head and wings mottled brown and black. The underparts bright yellow but with a conspicuous broad U-shaped black band across the breast. In flight there is much white visible in the sides and tip of the tail. The hind claw is greatly elongated.

DISTRIBUTION. Throughout West Africa in open country where grasses predominate.

HABITS. Usually seen in pairs. The flight is characteristic, flapping, then gliding with down-curved wings, revealing the white in the tail. These birds also run rapidly on the ground. Food consists mostly of insects but with seeds and other vegetable matter. Long-Claws breed during the rains, building the nest in a grass tuft, usually where the grass is long.

CALL. A shrill repeated call of "tew-eee" and more of a song in the breeding season.

BABBLERS, etc.
(*Timaliidae*)

The most typical members of this rather mixed family are the babblers that earn the name from their noisy habits. Smallish birds with fairly powerful bill and strong feet, plumages are very different in the different species.

40. Brown-Babbler (Plate VIII, 40)

Turdoides plebeja

The commonest babbler, but easily confused with the Blackcap Babbler.

RECOGNITION. Small medium. Greyish-brown in plumage rather darker above and paler below. The cheeks are noticeably pale, almost white and the crown is not darker than the back. (The Blackcap Babbler has dark cheeks and a black crown.) A conspicuous yellow eye and black bill and feet. The call is the best aid to identity.

DISTRIBUTION. Throughout West Africa apart from the thickest forest country.

HABITS. Almost always in small parties. The noise made by such a party attracts attention though the sound is not continuous; when one bird cries all join in. Feed chiefly on the ground amongst bushes on insects hidden beneath dead leaves. The flight usually a low glide to the nearest cover. The species is rather shy and patience is needed for a good view even though the chattering indicates the proximity of several birds. Breeding occurs in the rains, cup-shaped nests being made in low bushes. Often host to Levaillant's Cuckoo (No. 15).

CALL. A loud chattering "caa-caa-caa" like a rattle.

BULBULS

(*Pycnonotidae*)

Small medium birds, dull-coloured for the most part and subsisting on a mixed diet including berries and other fruits. Many are good songsters. The bill is usually slightly hooked at the tip.

41. Common Bulbul (*Plate IX, 41*)

Pycnonotus barbatus

There is no better-known bird in West Africa. It is found everywhere there is any human activity.

RECOGNITION. Small medium. A drab-coloured bird, upperparts earth brown, underparts dirty white. The slightly crested head and throat are darker, nearly black, distinguishing it from all other bulbuls.

DISTRIBUTION. Throughout West Africa.

HABITS. Usually in pairs or small parties. The flight is weak and of short duration. Perches conspicuously in bushes and small trees though occasionally seen on the ground. Small coloured fruits such as peppers are favourite foods; also insects. Remains alert throughout the day and calls at dawn all the year. On alighting the wings are often raised above the back while the bird calls quickly. Parties collect to scold hawks, snakes, etc. The prolonged breeding period is chiefly in the rains, nests being made in a wide variety of places.

CALL. A joyful little song, often represented as "Quick, doctor, Quick". When alighting, "toodleee, toodleee". Also a scolding "chit, chit, chit".

42. Yellow-throated Leaf-love   (*Plate IX, 42*)

pyrrhurus flavicollis

A noisy species, more colourful than most bulbuls, it is easily distinguished.

RECOGNITION. Medium size. Upperparts greenish-brown, underparts greyish but with bright yellow on chin and throat. A related species, the Simple Leaf-Love, has a pure white throat. The tail matches the upperparts and has no red in it, distinguishing this species from the somewhat similar Yellow-throated Olive Bulbul.

DISTRIBUTION. Widespread in West Africa, preferring well-wooded savannah country.

HABITS. Usually in pairs or small parties which seldom fly far. They spend much time in silent search for food but periodically the whole party breaks into a garrulous chattering that is quite unmistakable. This habit occurs mostly in the early mornings, but is specially noticeable in the rainy season when the species breeds. Nests are made in hedges and trees.

CALL. A harsh scolding chatter of "witcher, watcher, witcher, watcher" made in chorus.

FLYCATCHERS

(*Muscicapidae*)

A family of small birds of strictly insectivorous feeding habits. For this purpose the bill is typically flattened, short, wide at the base and has bristles to increase its efficiency in catching insects in flight. Many are very colourful, but some drab.

43. Spotted Flycatcher   (*Plate IX, 43*)

Muscicapa striata

A well-known bird in Europe that winters in Africa. Rather like the resident Pale Flycatcher.

RECOGNITION. Small size. Upperparts dull brown, underparts nearly white but with pronounced dark streaks on the breast. Paler markings on head and wings. (The Pale Flycatcher is a lighter brown above and has no breast streaks.) Its insect-catching flight is important in recognition.

DISTRIBUTION. Breeds throughout Europe. Most migrate into southern Africa for the winter, being common in West Africa on passage in "spring" and "autumn" though a few remain throughout the dry season.

HABITS. Usually solitary. It is best identified by its habit of perching, rather erect watching for insects, and then making a feeding sally with acrobatic flight to return to the same perch. This habit is much more pronounced in this species than in other flycatchers. The wings and tail are sometimes flicked open while the bird remains perched. Breeding does not concern us.

CALL. Usually a silent species in its winter quarters; but has a call of "ee-chit-chat".

44. Senegal Puffback Flycatcher   (*Plate IX, 44*)

Batis senegalensis

Not likely to be mistaken for any other bird, though the sexes differ a little.

RECOGNITION. Tiny. The male is essentially black and white. Crown, broad eye-stripe, upperparts and breast-band black: eyebrows, chin, throat and belly white. Tail also black and white. The female resembles the male in pattern but her eyebrow and breast-band are brown.

DISTRIBUTION. Throughout savannah country of West Africa, where trees are present.

HABITS. Usually seen in pairs, sometimes singly. Restless little birds catching most of their insect prey amongst the leaves of trees but sometimes flying after an insect well out into the air. They seldom

30

fly far at a time, and then tend to have a dipping flight. Breeding occurs at the end of the dry season. Tiny nests of grass, lichen and cobwebs are built low in trees.

CALL. Usually silent, but has a call of "you-beet" repeated several times.

45. Wattle-eye or Spectacled Flycatcher *(Plate IX, 45)*

Platysteira cyanea

A most attractive bird, both in appearance and in its song.

RECOGNITION. Small. The male glossy blue-black above, with white wing-bar; white below with a broad black breast band. There is a bright-red fleshy lobe ("wattle") over the eye, conspicuous at close range. The female resembles the male except that her throat and upper breast are dark purplish-brown, the rest of the underparts white.

DISTRIBUTION. Throughout West Africa in forest clearings and savannah except the arid north.

HABITS. Usually in pairs. Tends to remain in the cover of foliage and the jerky flight is used only to reach the next tree or bush. Hunts insects and occasionally flies out of cover to catch one with an audible snap of the bill. Reveals its presence by the sweet song, chiefly of the male. Bill snapping and wing noises are features of courtship; breeding occurs during the rains. The nest is a tiny affair of grass and lichens, placed low in a bush.

CALL. Characterised by a series of single, spaced, clear whistled notes, variously arranged, for example "so-doh-so-la-so".

46. Fagan's Paradise Flycatcher *(Plate X, 46)*

Tchitrea smithii

There are several rather similar Paradise Flycatchers in West Africa. Fagan's, common in western Nigeria, is typical, but rather local.

RECOGNITION. Small with long tail. The whole of the head glossy blue-black. The upperparts dull reddish-brown; the underparts a paler, brighter reddish-brown. Other Paradise flycatchers have these

31

two colours, blue-black and reddish-brown, in differing patterns and some have very long tails. (Birds from east of the Niger, though really the same species, have greyish backs and are called "Grey-backed Paradise Flycatchers".)

DISTRIBUTION. Paradise flycatchers as a group are widespread in West Africa, but different species are somewhat local.

HABITS. Usually singly or in pairs. Tend to keep in the cover of thick foliage and are more often heard than seen. When the notes are known it proves to be common. Strictly insectivorous, the prey is caught chiefly amongst leaves though sometimes the bird will fly into the open for it. Almost nothing is known of the breeding behaviour of this bird.

CALL. A tinkling call, like the ringing of tiny bells, representable as "diddle, diddle, diddle–diddle, diddle". Also a harsh alarm call of "whaaack, wa".

THRUSHES, WHEATEARS, CHATS, etc.

(*Turdidae*)

A very large family of somewhat diverse birds. All feed on a variety of small animals (insects, worms, snails, etc.) and fruits and have fairly long nearly straight bills. The sexes often quite distinct. Typically the young have spotted plumage. Many are migratory.

47. Kurrichane Thrush   (*Plate X, 47*)

Turdus libonyanus

The commonest true thrush of West Africa, not likely to be confused with any other bird.

RECOGNITION. Small medium. Sexes alike. Upperparts uniform brown, throat white with dark streaks, breast pale-brown, belly white. The flanks bright-orange showing clearly in flight. The bright-yellow bill is conspicuous.

DISTRIBUTION. Throughout West Africa, but slightly different races occur in different areas.

HABITS. Seen singly, in pairs or small parties. Feeds largely on the ground on worms, snails and insects, but also takes berries, etc.

When feeding it stands listening with slightly inclined head, then rushes forward to seize the prey. Feeds chiefly in the early morning and evening, and is not then shy if the observer is quiet. Often flies low with scolding cries. Its rich song is not heard during the driest months. It breeds chiefly in the rains, the nest being placed in a tree fork.

CALL. A rattling alarm call and another of "tchuck, tchuck, tchuck". The loud musical song, very like that of the European Song-thrush, comprises short, varied but repeated, phrases.

48. European Wheatear (*Plate X, 48*)

Oenanthe oenanthe

Several species of wheatear occur in West Africa, but this dry-season migrant from Europe is the most common.

RECOGNITION. Small medium. All wheatears are distinguishable at once as ground birds with a conspicuous white rump and black and white tail. Male and female are similar (in winter) with brownish back and buff underparts. The male develops breeding plumage with grey crown and back and black eye stripe before migration. Absence of any black on the throat and white extending down the sides of the tail distinguish this species from other wheatears.

DISTRIBUTION. On open ground throughout the drier parts of West Africa, from October to March.

HABITS. Solitary birds but becoming gregarious for migration. The flight, low over the ground, shows the dark wings, white rump and pied tail very clearly. Perches on small mounds and bobs and flirts its tail, usually calling at the same time. Chiefly insectivorous. Breeding does not concern us.

CALL. A quiet "wheet, chack, chack".

49. Whinchat (*Plate X, 49*)

Saxicola rubetra

One of the most numerous migrants from Europe, and quite distinctive despite plumage changes.

RECOGNITION. Small. Like the wheatear the male dons breeding plumage before migrating. On arrival the sexes are much alike; mottled brown above but with a conspicuous whitish eyebrow, and

33

reddish-buff throat. White shows in the side of the tail in flight. The breeding male has dark-brown cheeks, a reddish throat, pure white eyebrow and wing bar. The habit of perching conspicuously on top of a small bush aids recognition.

DISTRIBUTION. Throughout West Africa in open ground, particularly farms, from mid-October to early April.

HABITS. Usually solitary. Perch conspicuously, and show territorial behaviour (in the winter quarters) using the same bush day after day. Will fly to catch an insect and return to the same perch. Usually silent but display at an intruder of their own species with a metallic chinking call; this becoming more noticeable as the males develop breeding plumage. Breeding does not concern us.

CALL. A rather soft "tu-tink-tink". Its true song is not heard in Africa.

50. Snowy-headed Robin-Chat   (*Plate X, 50*)

Cossypha niveicapilla

The different species of Robin-Chats are shy birds, best known for their song.

RECOGNITION. Small medium. Sexes alike. All Robin-Chats have a plumage mainly dark blue-grey (slate) and reddish-orange. This species is distinguished by pure white over the crown. The cheeks, back, wings and central tail feathers are slate-blue, the underparts, rump and lateral tail feathers reddish-orange.

DISTRIBUTION. Widely distributed where there is thick vegetation, penetrating well into savannah near streams.

HABITS. Often seen in pairs, sometimes in small parties. The flight is quick, low and usually to the nearest cover. Through much of the year a shy species feeding on insects on the ground in thick bush, only revealing its presence by calling at dawn and dusk. In the rainy season, when breeding, it becomes much bolder and will drive off birds larger than itself. It now sings all day but still chiefly at dawn and dusk. Nests are built in various situations, sometimes in garden bushes.

CALL. A songster with a very beautiful range of liquid notes. Also mimics a number of other birds.

Plate IX

41   Common Bulbul

42   Yellow-throated Leaf-love

43   Spotted Flycatcher

44   Senegal Puffback Flycatcher

45   Wattle-eye or Spectacled Flycatcher

Plate X

46 Fagan's Paradise Flycatcher
47 Kurrichane Thrush
48 European Wheatear
49 Whinchat
50 Snowy-headed Robin-Chat

WARBLERS

(*Sylviidae*)

The members of this large family are mostly small dull-coloured birds, difficult to distinguish from each other. Nearly allied to thrushes they have slender straight bills and rather long legs for their size. Many are noted songsters, most easily distinguished by their voices.

51. Willow-Warbler

(*Plate XI, 51*)

Phylloscopus trochilus

A common migrant from Europe, though there are several, rarer, closely similar forms.

RECOGNITION. Small. Brownish-green above, nearly white below and with a prominent yellow eyebrow. The absence of bright yellow on throat or rump is an important distinction from close relatives. This group comprises birds of leafy trees, their habit of fluttering from twig to twig aiding recognition.

DISTRIBUTION. Throughout West Africa, wherever there are leafy trees, from October to March.

HABITS. Usually solitary, sometimes in parties, often with other birds. Searches the foliage of trees for insects and is never still. The weak fluttering flight employed at such times makes it difficult to comprehend the long migratory flight undertaken by this species. About February it starts singing, but full song is not heard in Africa. Breeding does not concern us.

CALL. The song is a trill of descending notes and the call, used at at all times, is a whistled "Who-it".

52. White-bellied Crombec

(*Plate XI, 52*)

Sylvietta flaviventris

Crombecs are shy but quite common warblers, more often heard than seen.

4—B.W.A.

RECOGNITION. Tiny. The tail is so short in crombecs that the group are easily recognised by this feature. This southern species is dull-green above with a pale eyebrow and whitish below, with yellow on the breast. Farther north the common species is the Senegal Crombec with grey upperparts and reddish-buff underparts.

DISTRIBUTION. In forest clearings and farms from Sierra Leone to Nigeria.

HABITS. A solitary and unobtrusive bird. By no means uncommon and enters gardens where it is sometimes seen away from cover, but usually it tends to keep in bushes from which its pleasing song may be heard. Insects are secured within foliage and its restlessness draws attention to the bird. Nests, made in the rainy season, are delicate affairs of fibres and spiders' web, suspended from a hanging twig.

CALL. Loud for the size of the bird: A rather squeaky "di-tweedle-di-tweedle- di-tweedle-di" repeated at intervals.

53. Grey-backed Camaroptera   (*Plate XI, 53*)

Camaroptera brevicaudata

Probably the most common resident warbler of West Africa.

RECOGNITION. Small. Head and back grey, the wings yellow-green. The underparts shade from grey on the throat to white on the belly. The tail is usually upturned sharply showing its pale underside; this habit and the call being the best guides to identification.

DISTRIBUTION. Throughout West Africa except the thickest forest.

HABITS. Usually in pairs. A rather shy species, heard much more often than seen but is not really difficult to see if the observer remains still. It hunts restlessly for insects in low vegetation with upturned tail. To sing it usually perches in the lowest branches of a large tree. In display it flies up and down vertically as though on a spring. The nest, made in the rainy season, is very difficult to find, as the bird draws large leaves right round and secures them to the nest.

CALL. A shrill alarm call of "beep" and the song (not heard in the driest months) of short bursts of "chip, chip, chip, chip, chip" repeated for long periods.

54. Red-faced Grass-Warbler   (*Plate XI, 54*)

Cisticola erythrops

Several different Grass-Warblers occur in West Africa, all so much alike they are most difficult to differentiate. This species is distinctive in plumage and song.

RECOGNITION. Small. All Grass-Warblers are small brownish birds with rounded fan-like tails having black or white spots near the tip of each feather. This species has uniform (not streaky) dull-brown upperparts, and the underparts nearly white. The distinctive feature is dull orange-red on the sides of the head. The birds become rather brighter during the rains, when they breed. The call is quite distinctive.

DISTRIBUTION. Throughout West Africa in forest clearings and southern savannah.

HABITS. In pairs or small parties. Nearly always found where long grasses and bushes intermix, and tends to remain low down in cover, except when singing. Will then climb to a conspicuous perch and utter the loud, forceful song; dipping down into cover if disturbed. Nests are concealed amongst grasses and have broad leaves drawn round them.

CALL. A series of evenly spaced loud notes "wink-wink-wink-cheeeer-cheeeer-cheeeer-wink-wink-wink".

55. Moustached Scrub-Warbler   (*Plate XI, 55*)

Melocichla mentalis

The largest West African warbler and might therefore be mistaken for a thrush.

RECOGNITION. Small medium. The upperparts earth brown becoming reddish on the forehead. Throat whitish but the rest of the underparts rufous-buff. A prominent black streak (the moustache) slants from the angle of the bill on to the white throat. A pale stripe behind the eye. Rather long tail, darker than the back.

DISTRIBUTION. Not yet recorded from the Gambia but throughout the rest of West Africa in savannah country.

HABITS. Usually in pairs. A rather shy species spending much time skulking in long grass, thickets and untidy corners of gardens. Morning and evening, especially after rain, it emerges from cover to sing richly from a conspicuous perch and can then be approached quite easily. The flight is low and only from cover to cover. Nests are made in the rainy season in grass tussocks or similar situations.

CALL. A sweet musical call, quite loud and repeated, of "tip-tip-tiɒ-twiddlee-iddlee-eeee".

SWALLOWS AND MARTINS

(Hirundinidae)

Small birds noted for their rapid, irregular, flight on long, pointed wings. Many have markedly forked tails. Feed exclusively on small insects caught in flight by the wide bill. Rather similar to swifts in form and habits but perch readily and usually have glossy blue-black over much of the upperparts, with white or reddish underparts.

56. European Swallow (Plate XII, 56)

Hirundo rustica

Vast numbers of this species migrate to Africa during the European winter. Very similar to the Gambia Swallow.

RECOGNITION. Small. Glossy blue-black above and mostly white below. Distinctive features are the red forehead and chin and broad blue-black band on the throat only clearly visible when the bird perches. The tail is deeply forked and shows white spots from above when spread. The Gambia Swallow, indistinguishable unless perched, has a red throat and only a narrow blue-black band between this and the white breast.

DISTRIBUTION. Throughout West Africa from late September to early April, but especially numerous at migration times.

HABITS. Strongly gregarious, particularly when migrating. Much time is spent in low flight, where insects are most numerous, playing fields and water being favourite places. Also settle in twittering parties on telegraph wires (but only rarely in trees). Readily drinking by dipping to a water surface in flight. A few stragglers remain through the year. Breeding does not concern us.

CALL. A twittering song and a sharp clicking call of "chip".

57. Ethiopian Swallow (*Plate XII, 57*)

Hirundo aethiopica

The most numerous swallow in Nigeria.

RECOGNITION. Small. Glossy deep-blue above and essentially all white below from chin to under the tail. The forehead is dark red, visible at close range. Whitish underparts without dark throat, and absence of red from crown or rump, are distinctive for this species of swallow.

DISTRIBUTION. Throughout the eastern half of West Africa and beyond into eastern Africa.

HABITS. Strongly gregarious. Although essentially a town species, also hunts insects above forest. Often perching in large numbers on telegraph wires along busy town streets. There is evidence of some local migration, numbers fluctuating considerably. Courtship display of the male involves hovering over the perched female. The nest, built of mud pellets, is often placed inside a room close below the roof. Breeding occurs in the early rains.

CALL. A sweet, canary-like song in the breeding season and a metallic call of "chip", like the last species.

58. Red-rumped Swallow (*Plate XII, 58*)

Hirundo rufula

This and the two following species of swallow all have red rumps, but this species is not difficult to distinguish.

RECOGNITION. Red, not only on the rump, but also across the back of the neck. All remaining upperparts glossy blue-black. The underparts from chin to vent nearly pure white but underside of the tail black. This obvious change from white to black at the base of the tail is distinctive for the species. The red colour is very pale in young birds.

DISTRIBUTION. Throughout the drier parts of West Africa, and subject to local migration.

HABITS. Sometimes met with in huge flocks, particularly in the valleys of large rivers, congregating where the river-bed is no more than damp during the dry season. Perches on wires and often roosts inside houses. Nests are made in the dry season. They are often placed beneath an overhanging river bank or below a bridge, and made of mud pellets. They are flask-shaped with long entrance tunnel.

CALL. A sweet twittering with a metallic quality.

59. Mosque Swallow (*Plate XII*, 59)

Hirundo senegalensis

Distinctly larger than all other swallows.

RECOGNITION. Small medium. Collar and rump rufous, the remaining upper parts very dark blue. The underparts also rufous (not nearly white as in the last species). The flight is distinctive, being much slower than other swallows'. It includes much gliding when the white underside to the inner half of the wing contrasts sharply with the blackish outer half. The tail-forks curve towards one another.

DISTRIBUTION. Throughout the savannahs of West Africa but subject to some migration.

HABITS. Usually in small flocks. The flight, usually rather high, is an alternation of flapping and gliding and seems lethargic for a swallow. Perch in bare trees as well as on wires. Quite early in the rains can be seen gathering mud pullets from roadside puddles but nest-building seems to be a slow process and occurs in a variety of places, hollow trees, beneath house-eaves or bridges, or below a cliff ledge. The nest is flask-shaped.

CALL. Quite distinctive and twanging, like the note of a toy trumpet.

60. Rufous-chested Swallow (*Plate XII*, 60)

Hirundo semirufa

Very like the Mosque Swallow and rather difficult to distinguish from it.

RECOGNITION. Small. Of the upperparts, only the rump is rufous (not the back of the neck as in the Mosque Swallow). The entire underparts are rufous. The remaining upperparts, including the upper half of the head down to the level of the eyes, deep-blue. Distinctly smaller than the Mosque Swallow and possessing exceptionally long tail-forks.

DISTRIBUTION. Throughout West Africa but subject to local migration.

HABITS. Usually in small flocks. The flight is sometimes low over open ground but is characteristically fairly high and involves more flapping and turning than gliding. Often perch in trees as well as on wires. Nests are made in the early rains in a variety of situations, notably below culverts and within porches and verandahs of houses. The nest is flask-shaped with long neck, made from mud pellets.

CALL. A twittering and high-pitched song, both on the wing and when perched. Lacks the twanging quality of the Mosque Swallow's call.

DRONGOS

(Dicruridae)

Drongos are aggressive black birds of medium size. Most species have characteristic "fish-like" tails, the feather tips curving outwards. They feed on quite large insects, the powerful hooked bill being well suited for this purpose.

61. Common or Glossy-backed Drongo   (Plate XIII, 61)

Dicrurus adsimilis

This typical drongo occurs everywhere in Africa outside the forest zone.

RECOGNITION. Medium size. Entirely black with strongly diverging feathers in the longish tail. The feathers of the mantle are glossy but not velvet-like as in the forest species. The two are so alike they cannot be distinguished in the field, except by habitat.

DISTRIBUTION. All Africa south of the Sahara except the rain-forests where it is replaced by the Velvet-mantled Drongo (*D. modestus*).

HABITS. Solitary, in pairs or small parties and sometimes very noisy. Perches to watch for insects which it takes both from the ground and in the air. The flight is both powerful and acrobatic. As day-light fails a drongo will ascend vertically a few feet, somersault and dive back with closed wings. Becomes very aggressive in the breeding season (the early rains) especially towards the Pied Crow. The nest is very small, for the size of the bird, suspended high in a tree between two twigs.

CALL. A harsh call of "wurchee-winchee". A loud whistling song, before dawn, occurs during the breeding season.

HELMET-SHRIKES

(Prionopidae)

A small family comprising strongly gregarious birds. All have stiff feathers on the forehead projecting forward over the nostrils and some are crested with similar stiff feathers.

62. Long-crested Helmet-Shrike (Plate XIII, 62)

Prionops plumata

An attractive pied bird always seen in small flocks.

RECOGNITION. Medium size. Quite unmistakable because of the black and white appearance, with long white crest on the head. White bars in the black wings are very conspicuous in flight and the flocking habit is an aid in recognition. A yellow fleshy wattle surrounding the eye is visible at close range.

DISTRIBUTION. Throughout wooded savannah of West Africa.

HABITS. Almost always in parties of 6 to 12 birds which fly, usually low, through the trees of orchard bush, farms and gardens. They search trees for insect food and also drop to the ground for it. Although silent in flight the birds may chatter together while foraging. They remain gregarious while breeding, several birds sharing in the building of a nest and feeding the young reared in it. Nests are made in low trees at the end of the dry season.

CALL. As well as chattering they have a loud alarm call of "chow, chow".

Plate XI

INCHES

51	Willow-Warbler	54	Red-faced Grass-Warbler
52	White-bellied Crombec	55	Moustached Scrub-Warbler
53	Grey-backed Camaroptera		

Plate XII

INCHES

56 European Swallow   59 Mosque Swallow

57 Ethiopian Swallow   60 Rufous-chested Swallow

58 Red-rumped Swallow

Plate XIII

INCHES

61 Common or Glossy-backed Drongo   64 Woodchat (European and Corsican)

62 Long-crested Helmet-Shrike   65 Long-tailed Shrike

63 Fiscal Shrike

Plate XIV

66 Scarlet-breasted Shrike or Gonolek	69 Black-crowned Tchagra or Bush Shrike
67 Bell-Shrike	70 Black-winged Oriole
68 Puff-back Shrike	

SHRIKES

(Laniidae)

A large family of birds with powerful hooked bills feeding mainly on insects but taking also eggs and young birds and even small mammals in their diet. From small to medium in size. Some are brightly coloured and some are migratory.

63. Fiscal Shrike (Plate XIII, 63)

Lanius collaris

Rather patchy in its distribution but common and conspicuous where it occurs; favouring gardens and compounds.

RECOGNITION. Small medium with long tail. Essentially black and white, though the rump is grey. All other upperparts black apart from a conspicuous white patch in the wing. Underparts white. The outer feathers of the graduated tail have white tips.

DISTRIBUTION. Very local but ranging from Sierra Leone to Cameroons.

HABITS. Usually in pairs. Very conspicuous birds perching on wires or on bush tops (unlike the Bell Shrike which is a shy pied shrike). From its perch it will fly to catch an insect and return again. Prey are not eaten on the wing but while perched, and sometimes a victim is impaled on a thorn for future attention. Breeding occurs at the start of the rains. Neat cup-shaped nests are placed in bushes.

CALL. Mostly silent birds but have a plaintive call of "tweeer" and a few musical notes heard at dawn in the breeding season.

64. Woodchat (European and Corsican) (Plate XIII, 64)

Lanius senator

The two closely similar races of this species are both common winter migrants to West Africa.

RECOGNITION. Small medium. The crown and nape are bright red-brown in contrast to the black forehead, eye stripe and back. The rump is whitish, the tail black and white. The wings are black with a conspicuous white shoulder patch. The underparts are white. The European race (64) has a small white patch in the wing absent in the Corsican race (64a).

43

DISTRIBUTION. Throughout West Africa from October to April in savannah country.

HABITS. A solitary species usually perching conspicuously on the top of a bush where it watches for insects though it sometimes hides within foliage. The rather undulating flight displays the pied plumage. Migration seems to continue slowly within West Africa, birds remaining in the north much longer than nearer the coast. Nesting does not concern us.

CALL. A silent species in Africa, though some report having heard it whistle.

65. Long-tailed Shrike (Plate XIII, 65)

Corvinella corvina

One of the most persistently noisy of all birds but rather drab in appearance.

RECOGNITION. Small medium with long tail. The plumage is streaky-brown on all upperparts, and buffish below with darker streaks. The tail is very long and strongly graduated. The bill is short, hooked and bright yellow. In flight the open wings show bright red-brown.

DISTRIBUTION. Savannah woodlands throughout West Africa.

HABITS. Almost always in parties of 6 to 12 or more. Perch in bushes and call noisily, the long tail being jerked up and down or rotated with a characteristic circular movement. Fruits are eaten as well as insects and small lizards, the food being taken largely on the ground. Usually fly from tree to tree individually, the others incessantly chattering. Movement on the ground is by such long hops, that the bird seems to bounce. Breeding occurs at the end of the dry season, nests being fairly large and placed in small trees.

CALL. A variety of harsh cries, something like "maaay we, may we, wait we——eah——eah——eah".

66. Scarlet-breasted Shrike or Gonolek (Plate XIV, 66)

Laniarius barbarus

A most strikingly coloured but rather shy bird, quite unmistakable.

44

RECOGNITION. Medium size. The crown and nape golden-yellow, all the rest of the upperparts and wings dark blue-black. Underparts bright red becoming buff under the tail. The call is important in recognition.

DISTRIBUTION. Throughout the savannah of West Africa including sandy coastal country.

HABITS. Solitary or in pairs. A shy bird that is much more often heard than seen. When the call is known patience is usually rewarded with a glimpse of the brightly coloured bird lurking in a bush. Sometimes more bold feeding on the ground in the open. The female answers the whistling call of the male with a harsh clicking noise. Breeding occurs in the rains, the deep cup-shaped nest being placed in a thick bush.

CALL. Has something of the quality of a whip being lashed. A double note sounding like "wheee, oo".

67. Bell-Shrike (*Plate XIV, 67*)

Laniarius ferrugineus

A most attractive bird, best known for its loud bell-like notes.

RECOGNITION. Medium size. Of particularly sleek appearance, all upperparts glossy black but with a white bar in the wing. The entire underparts white sometimes with a pink or buff wash on the breast. Rather long black tail.

DISTRIBUTION. From Sierra Leone to Cameroons, in savannah and forest clearings.

HABITS. Usually in pairs or small parties. Inclined to skulk within foliage and is therefore heard far more often than seen. The outstanding characteristic of this bird is its voice. The bell-like notes carry far and duets between two birds are commonly heard, sometimes more than two call in chorus. Often feed on the ground in garden corners. Though mainly insectivorous has a bad reputation for eating young birds. Breeding occurs in the rainy season, the nest a shallow structure placed low in a bush or tree.

CALL. The bell-like notes of "pooh-pooh-pooh" are unmistakable. A harsh repeated "tchak tchak, tchak" and a churring note as well.

68. Puff-back Shrike

Dryoscopus gambensis

So-called because of the ability of the male to raise the rump feathers to resemble a powder-puff.

RECOGNITION. Small medium. The sexes markedly different. The male has black crown and nape, streaky brown wings, the rump (unless the "puff" is raised) and tail very dark brown. The underparts white, the eye red. The female has grey crown and nape, the remaining upperparts pale brownish, the underparts orange-yellow.

DISTRIBUTION. Throughout the wooded savannahs of West Africa and also in forest clearings.

HABITS. Most often in pairs or parties. Usually fairly high in trees searching the foliage for insects, members of a group keeping up a scolding chatter to maintain contact with each other. This habit attracts attention and proves the species to be quite common though apt to be hidden. The rump puff-feathers are not often raised but are very striking when erected, as happens during display. Breeding occurs as the rains start, the nest being placed quite high in a tree fork.

CALL. A continuous scolding chatter of "tic, tchak, tchak, tchak" interspersed with "pi-chew".

69. Black-crowned Tchagra or Bush Shrike

Tchagra senegala (*Plate XIV, 69*)

Attracts attention by its melodious whistling despite inconspicuous colouring.

RECOGNITION. Small medium. Varying shades of brown on wings and back and all the underparts greyish-white. The head and tail are distinctive. The head has black crown and eye stripe separated by buff eyebrow. The tail is strongly graduated and has a white tip to all but the central feathers. In flight the wings appear reddish-brown and the tail patterning becomes conspicuous.

DISTRIBUTION. Throughout Africa south of the Sahara in fairly open country.

HABITS. Usually solitary or in pairs. In low bushes, by roadsides or in gardens, from which it sings, especially after rain. Flies low over the ground revealing the tail pattern. Feeds chiefly on the ground. A spectacular display flight, not confined to the breeding season, when the bird flies up singing and noisily cracking its wings, and then spirals down. Breeding occurs over long periods, the nest a cup in a low bush.

CALL. Most melodious and unmistakable. A series of clear separate whistled notes something like "fioo-tee-fioo-feee-whit-tew-whit".

ORIOLES

(*Oriolidae*)

A small family of birds with much golden-yellow in the plumage. They feed on insects and fruits gathered from large trees, within the foliage of which they remain concealed. All have clear rather similar musical whistles.

70. Black-winged Oriole (*Plate XIV, 70*)

Oriolus nigripennis

Very closely similar to the Black-headed Oriole, but quite distinct from all other birds.

RECOGNITION. Medium size. The whole of the head region black. The upperparts bright greenish-yellow but with black quills edging the wing. The underparts golden-yellow. The centre tail-feathers of this species are black, those of the generally similar Black-headed Oriole are green. Both have yellow-tipped outer tail feathers.

DISTRIBUTION. Chiefly in secondary forest from Sierra Leone to Cameroons.

HABITS. Usually in pairs; the two birds may be some distance apart but calling to each other regularly. Keep mostly to the thick foliage of tree-tops where the brilliant plumage is well concealed. Caterpillars and small fruits, such as figs, are favourite foods. The presence of these tree-top birds is revealed by the loud whistling call, rather like that of other orioles, suggesting the name "oriole". Little is known of the nesting of this species.

CALL. A loud and cheerful whistled call of "or-i-oh".

47

CROWS, MAGPIES, etc.

(*Corvidae*)

A family of fairly large birds, most of which have black or largely black plumage. They are strong fliers and have powerful slightly down-curved bills and strong legs and feet.

71. Pied Crow
(Plate XV, 71)

Corvus albus

There can be no mistaking this widespread bird.

RECOGNITION. Large. A white collar surrounding the neck, and the white extends from this collar well down to the belly. All other parts glossy black.

DISTRIBUTION. Somewhat local in occurrence, but throughout Africa south of the Sahara, in association with man.

HABITS. Strongly gregarious, flocks of over a hundred birds are not uncommon. The species roosts in favourite trees from which groups set off in the morning to forage for food. These parties join up during the day and large flights return to roost at sundown. Eats almost anything organic, e.g. carrion, eggs and young birds, insects, palm fruits. Despite size, indulges in aerobatic display flights. Fairly noisy in flight and when perched, but quieter on the ground. Breeding in separated pairs occurs in the early rains, a large stick nest being built high in a tree or even a high building such as a minaret of Kano Mosque!

CALL. A "language" of different calls, the one most used may be written "Kaa, Kaa".

72. Piapiac or Black Magpie
(Plate XV, 72)

Ptilostomus afer

Sufficiently distinctive in form and habits to be unmistakable. The name Piapiac is derived from the call.

RECOGNITION. Medium large with very long tail. The plumage appears entirely glossy black though the wings are actually very dark

48

brown and seem pale in flight. The very long tail is strongly graduated. The bill is black in adults, red in young birds.

DISTRIBUTION. Throughout the savannahs of West Africa, particularly where Borassus palms occur.

HABITS. Always in small flocks. A tame bird, that can be approached closely with ease. Feeds on the ground, then retires scolding noisily into a tree if disturbed, but drops down to the ground again when the intruder has passed. Often feeds amongst domestic animals and sometimes perches on their backs. The flight is rather slow, despite the rapid wing-beat, with the long tail trailing. The shrill call is heard particularly at dawn and dusk. Breeding occurs at the end of the dry season, nests often being made in palm trees.

CALL. A shrill repeated "pee-ip, pee-ip".

STARLINGS, etc.

(Sturnidae)

A large and diverse family of mostly medium-sized birds. Fruits as well as insects and other small animals are included in the diet. Most species nest in holes in trees.

73. Amethyst or Violet-backed Starling (Plate XV, 73)

Cinnyricinclus leucogaster

The male a really beautiful bird but the female dull-coloured and not easily recognised unless with the male.

RECOGNITION. Small medium. The male has the entire upperparts, throat and upper breast a brilliant metallic purple. The rest of the underparts pure white. The female is dark-brown above with paler edges to the feathers and whitish underparts heavily streaked with dark-brown.

DISTRIBUTION. Throughout West Africa, subject to migratory movements, and somewhat local.

HABITS. Strongly gregarious, sometimes huge flocks are encountered in the evening, either in flight or perched in trees. The flight is fast and straight. Feeds largely on fruits and also insects. The migratory movements are not yet understood and are possibly more of a dispersal from breeding areas to where food is abundant. Nests

49

are made by lining tree holes, breeding occurring at the start of the rains.

CALL. A rather querulous "keeow, keeow". Also a thrush-like whistle.

74. Purple Glossy Starling   (*Plate XV, 74*)

Lamprocolius purpureus

A number of Glossy Starlings occur in West Africa, easy to recognise as such, but very difficult to distinguish from each other. The different species tend to occur in different types of country and this is often the best guide to identity.

RECOGNITION. Medium size. The dark plumage is shot with iridescent metallic colour, purplish on the head and all the underparts, greenish on the wings and back. The eye is a conspicuous golden yellow.

DISTRIBUTION. Through West Africa especially southern savannahs where good-sized trees occur. Subject to some migratory movements.

HABITS. A gregarious species outside the breeding season, usually in small flocks, sometimes larger ones. Feed mostly on the ground and are then fairly silent but when perching in trees chatter together noisily and so attract attention. The wings produce a whirring sound during flight, very noticeable when several fly together. Nests are made in tree holes in the early rainy season.

CALL. A rather nasal twanging kind of call interspersed with squeaks and whistles.

75. Chestnut-winged Starling   (*Plate XV, 75*)

Onychognathus fulgidus

Despite the name this appears to be an all-black bird. Care must be taken to distinguish it from a Drongo (No. 61).

RECOGNITION. Medium size with fairly long tail. A very sleek bird. The plumage of the male is glossy black except for a patch of reddish-brown on the wings not noticeable unless the open wing is seen closely. The female differs in having a streaky grey head. The tail has no suggestion of a fork as in the Drongo. A powerful, slightly hooked bill and red eye.

Plate XV

INCHES

♀

74

73

♂

75

72

71

INCHES

71 Pied Crow

72 Piapiac or Black Magpie

73 Amethyst or Violet-backed Starling

74 Purple Glossy Starling

75 Chestnut-winged Starling

Plate XVI

INCHES

76   Senegal or Yellow White-eye   79   Splendid Sunbird

77   Pygmy Long-tailed Sunbird   80   Olive-bellied Sunbird

78   Copper Sunbird

DISTRIBUTION. Throughout the forest zone of West Africa, especially in clearings and near hills.

HABITS. In pairs or small parties. The flight is undulating due to the bird's habit of closing the wings momentarily after every score or so of beats. Usually seen in the tree-tops where it feeds on fruits, seeds and insects. Draws attention, especially in the evenings, by its calling. Almost nothing is known of its nesting behaviour, though tree holes are used and breeding occurs in the rains.

CALL. A loud clear whistle of "tew-whee-yew".

WHITE-EYES

(*Zosteropidae*)

A family of very small birds characterised by a ring of whitish minute feathers surrounding the eye. The bill is slender and very slightly curved.

76. Senegal or Yellow White-eye   (*Plate XVI, 76*)

Zosterops senegalensis

Difficult to distinguish from the Green White-eye (*Z. virens*) but the latter only occurs at high altitude in West Africa.

RECOGNITION. Tiny. Bright yellow-green above, bright yellow below. A white eye ring. Brownish feathers in the wings and tail. The delicate bill is shining black. Forest birds are rather less brightly coloured than those from the savannah.

DISTRIBUTION. Throughout the whole of West Africa where thick-foliaged trees occur.

HABITS. Usually in small parties the birds calling to one another. Keep largely within the foliage of shrubs and trees where they are well hidden. Might be thought uncommon till the call is known when they prove to be frequent visitors to gardens. Search the foliage for small insects as food, also taking small seeds and fruits. The flight is weak and undulating, never prolonged. Breeding occurs in the early rains. The nest is a tiny cup suspended between two twigs.

CALL. A thin, but quite loud, squeaking call keeps a party together. Also a shrill song.

SUNBIRDS

(*Nectariniidae*)

A family of very small birds, the males of most species having some iridescent metallic plumage at least in the breeding season, the females being dull. In some species the males have a drab "eclipse" plumage also. Sunbirds have long curved beaks and feed with the aid of a tubular tongue on nectar; they also take tiny insects visiting flowers. Sunbirds usually perch to feed, but can also hover to do so. They suspend their domed nests in a characteristic way. Very active birds with shrill voices. Many species are common garden visitors.

77. Pigmy Long-tailed Sunbird   (*Plate XVI, 77*)

Hedydipna platura

The breeding male is a beautiful and unmistakable bird.

RECOGNITION. Tiny with long tail. The breeding male has the head, throat and upperparts metallic green, the remaining underparts very bright yellow. The tail feathers are blackish and the two central ones greatly elongated and enlarged at the tip. The female is grey-brown above, pale yellow below. From about April to September the male resembles the female.

DISTRIBUTION. Throughout the savannahs of West Africa.

HABITS. Usually solitary or in pairs. Like all sunbirds, a very active species, never remaining long in one tree, whose flowers it examines in quick succession. Acacia and Bombax trees are favourites. The flight is rapid and darting. There is evidence of some local migration. Breeding occurs in the dry season. The domed nest is made of fine grass, lichens and spiders' web, has a side entrance with "porch" and is suspended from a twig.

CALL. A high-pitched "cheek" and also a trilling song.

78. Copper Sunbird   (*Plate XVI, 78*)

Cinnyris cupreus

The male in breeding plumage is unmistakable. The female and "eclipse" male are much like other female sunbirds.

RECOGNITION. Small. The breeding male appears entirely glossy black, but with a coppery sheen over the entire head and violet iridescence on the breast and mantle. The female is greenish-brown above and dull yellowish below, with black tail. The male's "eclipse" plumage, like the female's, but usually retaining some black feathers; is met from about November to January. The breeding plumage is then assumed gradually, being completed about March.

DISTRIBUTION. Common throughout West African tree savannah.

HABITS. Met with singly, in pairs or small parties. Very active, searching flowers and piercing their bases to get both nectar and insects. The flight is very rapid, irregular in direction and includes hovering. An incessant chatter is usually maintained by the birds. Breeding occurs towards the end of the rains, the domed nest suspended from a low branch in a bush and with a wispy "beard" below.

CALL. Not very distinctive, merely a rather sharp, rapid sustained clicking.

79. Splendid Sunbird   (*Plate XVI, 79*)

Cinnyris coccinigaster

The male may well be considered the most beautiful of all sunbirds.

RECOGNITION. Small, though appreciably larger than the Copper Sunbird. The male appears black but has vivid metallic sheens, purple on the head, green on back and wing-coverts. The breast has a close barring of blue and scarlet. The female has little to distinguish her from other female sunbirds apart from larger size and slightly streaky underparts. Rather long curved bill.

DISTRIBUTION. Chiefly in wooded savannahs of West Africa, but extending to secondary-forest clearings.

HABITS. Solitary or in pairs, but associating with other sunbirds. Often resorts to tree-tops as well as feeding at flowers of garden shrubs. It perches on top of a good-sized tree to sing, having a more distinctive voice than most sunbirds. There is no "eclipse" plumage, but some evidence of local migration. Breeding seems to be irregular and protracted. The domed nest is noteworthy for concealment, thick lining and absence of "beard".

53

CALL. A loud melodious song of separate notes becoming lower in pitch, with longer intervals between them.

80. Olive-bellied Sunbird   (*Plate XVI, 80*)

Cinnyris chloropygius

A pity this beautiful bird should be dubbed with such a dull name, referring to the only drab part of its plumage.

RECOGNITION. Tiny. The male has the entire head, throat and back vivid metallic green. The breast is scarlet, the belly dull yellowish-green, the wings brown, the tail blackish. The female is a drab greenish-brown above, dull yellow below with wings and tail like those of the male.

DISTRIBUTION. Forest clearings and river valleys from Sierra Leone to Cameroons, though slightly different races occur.

HABITS. Seen singly, in pairs, or small parties and fairly tame. One of the most active little birds, remaining so throughout the heat of the day. Hovers at flowers more than other sunbirds and keeps up an incessant chatter while feeding. Seen in fairly thick bush as well as gardens and clearings. Breeding occurs towards the end of the rains; the nest, a domed structure with hanging "beard", is suspended fairly low in a bush.

CALL. An incessant twittering and also a loud call of "cheep-cheep".

81. Scarlet-breasted Sunbird   (*Plate XVII, 81*)

Chalcomitra senegalensis

Probably the most common sunbird of savannah country.

RECOGNITION. Small. The male has crown and upper throat metallic blue-green, lower throat and breast scarlet, and almost all the rest of the body velvety brown-black. At close range the scarlet feathers can be seen to bear a blue bar near the tip. The female is dull-brown above and on the throat, with streaky yellow-white on breast and belly.

DISTRIBUTION. Different races occur throughout the savannahs of Africa.

HABITS. Usually in pairs or small parties. Seems to prefer flowering trees such as Bombax to lower shrubs. A very active species, birds of a party chasing one another noisily especially just before the breeding season. Will sometimes catch an insect in flight, in flycatcher style, returning to the same perch. Breeding occurs during the rains. The nest of the usual sunbird pattern, rather larger than most, and without beard.

CALL. The usual "cheep" and "tick, tick" of sunbirds and also some clear notes.

82. Green-headed or Olive-backed Sunbird

Cyanomitra verticalis (Plate XVII, 82)

One of the few sunbirds in which the female has iridescent feathers.

RECOGNITION. Small, though large for a sunbird. The male has the head and throat vivid metallic blue-green, the upperparts and wings unglossed yellow-green and the breast and belly dull lead-grey. The female differs from the male in lacking metallic feathers on the throat, being grey right up to the chin, the whole underside paler than in the male.

DISTRIBUTION. Forest clearings, river valleys and southern savannah right across West Africa.

HABITS. Usually in pairs. Works quickly and diligently over flowering shrubs and the like in search of food, which is mainly small insects and spiders but also some nectar. Seldom hovers. More silent than most other sunbirds. Breeding seems to have occurred in all the rainy months. The nest is a rather untidy affair, domed and suspended from a twig with wisps of material hanging from it.

CALL. Several different notes, the most characteristic a rather plaintive "tee-eep".

83. Collared Sunbird (Plate XVII, 83)

Anthreptes collaris

Another sunbird in which both sexes possess metallic plumage.

RECOGNITION. Tiny. The male bright metallic green from head to tail on the upperparts and on the throat. A narrow purple band on the breast, the rest of the underparts bright yellow. The female like the male above but underparts from chin to tail dull yellow. The male is a little like the male Yellow-bellied Sunbird, but this species is pale yellow below and the female is drab, without any metallic feathers.

DISTRIBUTION. Common in secondary forest clearings from most of tropical Africa.

HABITS. Most often in pairs. Prefer the lower vegetation of forest clearings and often visit gardens. The diet consists mainly of insects, the relatively short bill and tongue being less suited to nectar feeding. Breeding occurs in the rains, mainly late in the wet season. The domed nest is suspended, rather higher from the ground than that of most sunbirds, usually amongst scrambling leafy lianas.

CALL. A reedy call of "pseep". Also a sweet song in the breeding season, mostly in the early morning.

FINCHES, BUNTINGS AND SPARROWS

(Fringillidae)

A large family of small-sized birds adapted for seed-eating by having short stout conical bills. Grass seeds, including small cereals, are favourite foods.

84. Yellow-fronted Canary   (Plate XVII, 84)

Serinus mozambicus

A favourite cage bird, not difficult to recognise in the field.

RECOGNITION. Small. Most noticeable are the bright yellow underparts. The crown grey, the head strongly marked with yellow and black, the back dull green, the rump pale yellow, conspicuous in flight. The conical beak is important to notice.

DISTRIBUTION. Different races occur throughout the tree-savannah country of all Africa.

HABITS. Strongly gregarious when not breeding. Feed on the ground in flocks, chiefly on small seeds. The flight is usually low and rather jerky displaying the pale yellow rump. A tame species and therefore easily trapped. Attention is often drawn to the bird by its habit of perching in a tree and singing frequently. The breeding season is ill-defined, the nest a compact cup placed in a tree fork some distance out from the trunk.

CALL. A sweet song of trilling notes that will be familiar to most, from caged specimens.

85. Rock-Bunting (*Plate XVII, 85*)

Fringillaria tahapisi

A common bird of savannah country showing a preference for places with bare rock outcroppings.

RECOGNITION. Small. Reddish-brown in general body colour, with markings of darker brown above. The head is the distinctive region, being strongly patterned in black and white and with grey on chin and throat. (The related House Bunting has a streaky grey head.) The bill, though conical, is relatively slender.

DISTRIBUTION. From Sierra Leone eastward into savannahs of the rest of Africa. Subject to some migratory movement.

HABITS. Met singly or in pairs, though sometimes flocking. Tame and easy of approach, not flying far when disturbed. Feed mainly on the ground but usually perch near the top of a small tree to sing and thus become conspicuous. Although birds of dry country they are attracted to water. Breeding occurs in the dry season. The nest is a shallow grass cup on or near the ground, amongst boulders.

CALL. A thin, shrill call of "tweet-tweedle-tweedle-tweet", much repeated.

86. Grey-headed Sparrow (*Plate XVIII, 86*)

Passer griseus

Usually met with amongst human habitations or on farms.

RECOGNITION. Small. The grey head shades to brown on the back and a more reddish rump. Wings patterned red-brown and earth-brown. Underparts greyish-white. Unlike most sparrows, the sexes are alike. Bill black in breeding season, pale-brown in off-season. Forest zone birds belong to a brighter race than savannah birds.

DISTRIBUTION. Throughout almost all Africa south of the Sahara. Essentially a town bird; very common in the north, but rather more sporadic in the south.

HABITS. In pairs or in flocks. Feed mostly on the ground, especially amongst droppings of domestic animals, taking insects as well as seeds and refuse. Less conspicuous than town sparrows of other parts of the world. Perch in trees to sing and also roost in them or on buildings. Breeding occurs chiefly late in the rains, but also sporadically through the year. The nest is very untidy, domed and placed in a tree or under a house roof.

CALL. The commonest note is a loud "cheeerp", much repeated.

WEAVERS, WAXBILLS, etc.

(Ploceidae)

A very large family of medium-sized to very small birds. Typical forms have conical bills and feed largely on grass seeds. One section of the family weave elaborate nests and suspend them in trees, bushes or grasses. Most of the rest build rather untidy domed nests chiefly of grasses. In many the sexes are very different and some have seasonal plumage changes. Few have distinctive calls.

87. Scaly-fronted Weaver   (Plate XVIII, 87)

Sporopipes frontalis

Stands rather apart from other members of the family and resembles a small sparrow.

RECOGNITION. Tiny. Upperparts patterned shades of brown, nearly orange across the back of the neck. The underparts whitish. The head is quite distinctive; the crown covered by dark feathers with white tips giving a scaly appearance, the greyish cheeks and white throat separated by black moustache stripes.

DISTRIBUTION. Right across Africa just south of the Sahara, in dry savannah country.

HABITS. Usually seen in flocks and often associating with other small weavers. A fairly tame species feeding on the ground in farms and gardens. Roost in parties in bushes and will utilise old nests for this purpose if available. Breeding occurs in the dry season, large untidy nests of dry grass heads being placed in low bushes.

CALL. A twittering little song.

Plate XVII

INCHES

81   Scarlet-breasted Sunbird

82   Green-headed or Olive-backed
      Sunbird

83. Collared Sunbird

84   Yellow-fronted Canary

85   Rock-Bunting

Plate XVIII

INCHES

86 Grey-headed Sparrow	89 Village Weaver
87 Scaly-fronted Weaver	90 Spectacled Weaver
88 Chestnut-and-Black Weaver	

Plate XIX

91	Red-headed Weaver or Red-headed Malimbe	94	Bronze Mannikin
92	Red-headed Dioch	95	Grey-crowned Negro-Finch
93	Yellow-mantled Whydah		

Plate XX

96 Senegal Fire-Finch	99 Senegal Combassou or Indigo-Finch
97 Orange-cheeked Waxbill	100 Pin-tailed Whydah
98 Red-cheeked Cordon-bleu	

88. Chestnut-and-Black Weaver (*Plate XVIII, 88*)

Cinnamopteryx castaneofuscus

Somewhat of a problem species, now thought to be a colour variant of an all-black species occurring farther east.

RECOGNITION. Small. Sexes very different. The male black on head, breast, wings and tail, most of the body feathers being a rich red-brown (chestnut). The female is mottled dark-brown above and dull yellowish-grey below with a reddish tinge on the flanks. Both sexes have a pale-yellow eye, conspicuous in the male.

DISTRIBUTION. Very numerous in forest country from Sierra Leone to the Niger, being replaced from there eastward by Viellot's Black Weaver with entirely black male.

HABITS. Strongly gregarious. Feed in groups in bushes and trees, often on abandoned farms. Roost in vast flocks with other weavers in tall grasses during the dry season. The first rains start breeding operations. Nests are built in colonies, often in a tree in a village, sometimes in company with Village Weavers. Nesting is sometimes over water. Elaborate courtship display exhibited, the male hanging below the entrance to the domed nest.

CALL. A most unmusical mixture of chirpings and wheezes.

89. Village Weaver (*Plate XVIII, 89*)

Plesiositagra cucullatus

The best-known of all true weavers.

RECOGNITION. Small medium. The breeding male has a black head, a black V-marking across the shoulders and most of the rest of the plumage golden-yellow. The female is mottled dull-green above and pale-yellow below. Both sexes have a powerful black bill. The male moults to resemble the female when not breeding in arid country but seems not to change in forest country.

DISTRIBUTION. Throughout West Africa and beyond.

HABITS. Strongly gregarious, whether feeding, flying, roosting or nesting. Feed partly on insects as well as grass seeds. Can be very destructive of palms when nest-building. Breeding occurs over much of the year but is associated with rain. The male weaves the nest shell, and displays below its entrance. If the female accepts him, she lines

59

the nest and lays into it. A breeding colony is very noisy but periodically the noise ceases abruptly, and the birds may fly away temporarily. Favourite trees, usually in a village, carry a colony for years in succession; a colony may contain several hundred birds.

CALL. Not distinctive, but consisting of wheezes and chirpings.

90. Spectacled Weaver   (*Plate XVIII, 90*)

Hyphanturgus brachypterus

Takes its name from the black stripe, possessed by both sexes, passing through the eye.

RECOGNITION. Small. The male has a black throat and eye stripe, the rest of the head and upper breast orange. The upperparts are uniform yellow-green and the remaining underparts bright yellow. The female is generally similar but lacks the black throat and orange feathers. Both are confusable with other weavers unless seen together.

DISTRIBUTION. Throughout West Africa, in tree savannah and forest clearings.

HABITS. Usually in pairs, sometimes small parties. Remarkable for being non-gregarious, though roosting in mixed flocks of weavers in the dry season. Feed chiefly on insects which are sought in tree and bush foliage. A tame species, sometimes nesting beside houses. Breeding occurs during the rains, the nest with bottom entrance is usually placed in thick foliage for concealment. The male does most of the nest construction and sings while doing so.

CALL. Quite distinctive but can only be described as a series of clicks and long-drawn-out wheezes.

91. Red-headed Weaver or Red-headed Malimbe

Malimbus rubricollis   (*Plate XIX, 91*)

Representative of the Malimbes, a group of scarlet and black weavers.

RECOGNITION. Small medium. The male has crimson-scarlet forehead, crown, nape and sides of neck. All the rest of the plumage black. The female differs very slightly in having a black forehead.

DISTRIBUTION. Common in forest clearings from Sierra Leone to Cameroons and beyond.

HABITS. Usually in pairs, sometimes in small parties. A pair often fly rather jerkily from one tree-top to another calling to each other. The food is mainly insects obtained from the trunks and major boughs of large trees. The birds climb about such surfaces with great agility, sometimes head down. Relatively little is known of the breeding habits of this bird despite its being quite common. Nests are usually built in a small group of three or so and sometimes interlace. The nest is shaped like an inverted sock, placed high in a tree and made untidily of woven fibres.

CALL. A jingling little call, sounding like "pee, chink——pee, chink" together with wheezing notes.

92. Red-headed Dioch   (*Plate XIX, 92*)

Quelea erythrops

One of two rather similar species notorious for damaging cereal crops.

RECOGNITION. Small. The breeding male has a bright-red head, contrasting with the mottled brown ("sparrowy") upperparts and buff underparts. The female and the non-breeding male lacking the red head, are not very distinctive. The bill is black. In the much more destructive Black-faced Dioch (*Quelea quelea*) the breeding male has a black face and both sexes have a red bill at all seasons.

DISTRIBUTION. From Sierra Leone to Cameroons in tree savannah and forest clearings.

HABITS. Strongly gregarious at all times, flocks of several hundreds are commonly seen. (Flocks of several millions of the Black-faced Dioch have been reported!) Feed almost exclusively on small grass seeds including those of millet, rice and guinea-corn. Being fairly tame they are not easily scared from crops. A flock will rise, chattering, and with whirring wings, to fly as a compact group. Breeding occurs during the rains. Nests are built in colonies usually in grasses. The nest is rounded, unlined, with side entrance.

CALL. Chattering that is not distinctive.

93. Yellow-mantled Whydah
(Plate XIX, 93)

Coliuspasser macrourus

The breeding male is one of West Africa's most distinctive common birds.

RECOGNITION. Small with long tail. The breeding male is entirely black apart from a conspicuous, triangular, bright-yellow shoulder patch. The long tail is noticeably wide. The female "sparrowy" and only readily recognised when with the male. When in eclipse plumage the male becomes like the female but retains some of the yellow shoulder feathers.

DISTRIBUTION. Throughout the whole of tropical Africa outside the rain forests. Subject to local migration.

HABITS. Usually seen singly or in pairs. Feed on grass seeds and insects. The breeding male perches on tops of grasses, bushes and small trees and seems embarrassed by the long tail. The head-feathers may be puffed out. Short flights are rather bouncing. The female tends to remain concealed in long grass. Most often seen on ground subject to flooding especially near villages. Breeding occurs in the rains. Nests are rather flimsy, usually built in short grass close above flood water.

CALL. A rather soft "chee-ee" is uttered by the perched male.

94. Bronze Mannikin
(Plate XIX, 94)

Spermestes cucullatus

A particularly tame species that attracts attention despite very small size.

RECOGNITION. Tiny. Throat, head and upperparts are mainly very dark brown, the underparts white. Brown and white alternate in bars on the flanks and rump. Spots of bronze-green on the wing give this species its name. The related Blue-billed Mannikin is black and white (not dark-brown) and has a pale-bluish bill.

DISTRIBUTION. Throughout the whole of West Africa and beyond.

HABITS. Gregarious, and even while nesting several pairs may build close together. Feed in flocks on the ground or on grasses and when disturbed do not fly far. On grass stems they hang upside-down and move acrobatically collecting seed. Fond of bathing, even in road puddles. Seldom silent in flight. Families roost in old nests, an astonishing number of birds packing into a small space. Breeding occurs chiefly during the rains. The untidy nest is made rapidly by both birds gathering grass heads to form a loose rounded structure with side entrance, in shrubs and creepers near houses.

CALL. Twittering that is not distinctive.

95. Grey-crowned Negro-Finch (*Plate XIX*, *95*)

Nigrita canicapilla

The most common of the Negro-Finches and easily distinguished.

RECOGNITION. Small. This high-perching species appears entirely black when seen from below. Actually the upperparts from crown to rump are grey and separated from the black forehead by a white line. The black wings have numerous small white spots. A conspicuous pale-yellow eye. In the related Pale-fronted Negro-Finch (*Nigrita luteifrons*) the forehead is whitish, the wings unspotted and the female grey below.

DISTRIBUTION. In forest country from Guinea to Cameroons and beyond.

HABITS. Usually solitary or in pairs, but small flocks occur in the evening. A bird of garden tree-tops where its dark silhouette and plaintive song are quite distinctive. Feed largely on palm-nut husks and seldom come near the ground. Often remain conspicuously perched for some while without moving. Breeding occurs in the rains. The nest is fairly large and untidy, constructed of fibres and dead leaves with side entrance. It is often placed in a liana.

CALL. A very plaintive call of separate notes, commonly "whooeee ——whooeee——whoo".

96. Senegal Fire-Finch (*Plate XX*, *96*)

Lagonosticta senegala

Probably the tamest bird in West Africa. One of several rather similar species.

RECOGNITION. Tiny. The male looks at first to be all crimson, with red bill. The tail, however, is black and the sides of the breast have white flecks and the wings are brownish. The female is mostly brown but has crimson in front of the eyes and also upper tail coverts. This is the only Fire-Finch in which the male has the entire head crimson.

DISTRIBUTION. Widespread throughout West Africa but mainly in the drier parts.

HABITS. Usually in small flocks, sometimes pairs. Mostly seen on the ground, picking up seeds as food. Rather weak in flight, it seldom moves far at a time. So tame that it will enter verandahs and even rooms and frequently nests in roof-thatch and the grass walls of native houses. Breeding occurs over a long period but mostly in the rains. The rounded, domed nest is constructed loosely of grasses copiously lined with feathers.

CALL. A piping call that is not distinctive.

97. Orange-cheeked Waxbill (*Plate XX*, 97)

Estrilda melpoda

A singularly attractive, and very common little bird.

RECOGNITION. Tiny. The orange-red cheeks and bill are the distinctive features of this species. Other important points are the red rump, blackish tail, grey head and back, brownish wings and pale-greyish underparts with a yellowish wash on the belly.

DISTRIBUTION. Throughout the whole of West Africa wherever grasses are abundant.

HABITS. Almost always in flocks, sometimes of large numbers. Feed mainly amongst grasses, climbing acrobatically on the stems with a sideways flicking of the tail. Usually move in compact groups, calling as they fly. Being quite tame they are easily approached and make good cage birds. Often associate with other small weavers. Breeding occurs chiefly in the rains; an elaborate courtship behaviour has been described. Rounded nests of grass heads with lateral funnelled opening are placed low in grass clumps, sometimes almost on the ground.

CALL. A shrill twittering keeps the flock together. Also a breeding-season song.

98. Red-cheeked Cordon-bleu   (*Plate XX, 98*)

Uraeginthus bengalus

Tiny size and pale-blue colouring predominating make this a charming bird, and a cage favourite.

RECOGNITION. Tiny. The sexes much alike though the male alone has the crimson cheek patch that distinguishes this species from other Cordon-bleus. Plumage otherwise bright pale blue and earth-brown. Blue occurs on the rump, face, breast and flanks; the crown, back, wings and belly brownish. The tail is relatively long and graduated.

DISTRIBUTION. Right through the drier parts of West Africa.

HABITS. Almost always in small flocks. Feed on the ground in gardens and on roadsides on grass seeds and the like, moving with minute hops. When so doing it is easily approached and usually only flies into adjacent bushes if driven off. Associates with other small weavers. Breeding occurs chiefly late in the rains. Untidy grass nests, with rounded side opening, are usually placed in thorny bushes at no great height. Like some other small weavers, nests are often associated with wasps' nests and thus gain added protection.

CALL. A plaintive little squeaking note, not very distinctive.

99. Senegal Combassou or Indigo-Finch   (*Plate XX, 99*)

Hypochera chalybeata

Representative of a group of birds, so alike that even in the hand they take much distinguishing.

RECOGNITION. Small. The breeding male is a nearly black bird, with distinct blue gloss, and a very pale bill. The wings and tail contain black quill feathers. (Other combassous have a green or purple gloss, or brownish quill feathers.) The female is a dull sparrowy bird and the male resembles her while in the eclipse plumage.

DISTRIBUTION. The different combassous are found throughout West Africa especially the drier parts.

HABITS. Usually in small flocks. So little is known about these tame common birds they would repay study. If possible such study should include collecting specimens for exact identification. Combassous feed on seeds and insects. It has now been established that they are parasitic, laying their eggs in the nests of waxbills, but sometimes rear their own young when in captivity, suggesting that the parasitic habit is relatively new. Polygamy is said to occur.

CALL. Usually silent, but the male has a shrill song in the breeding season.

100. Pin-tailed Whydah (Plate XX, 100)

Vidua macroura

The fantastic tail of the breeding male attracts attention from the most casual observer.

RECOGNITION. Small, with long tail in the male. The breeding male has a pied plumage. Crown, back and tail are glossy blue-black, underparts, back of the neck and rump white, wings black and white, the central tail feathers greatly elongated, reaching 10 inches in some birds. The bill bright pink. The female is "sparrowy" but has the distinctive bill. The male in eclipse resembles the female but usually keeps some black and some white feathers.

DISTRIBUTION. Throughout most of Africa south of the Sahara.

HABITS. In flocks when not breeding. At these times dividing their time between silent ground-feeding in farms and gardens and rather noisy preening assembly in trees. The species breeds during the rains, and the polygamous males perform elaborate courtship flights which draw attention. They appear to stand in the air on the long tail, poised by a flicking of the wings. This, too, is a parasitic species, utilising the nests of Waxbills for egg deposition.

CALL. A sharp chirping note and a shrill clicking song during courtship.